TALES FROM
TIME-OUT

By
Henry J. Roth, Ph. D.

Illustrations By
Lorraine Sharon Roth

Cover, illustrations & interior design by Lorraine Sharon Roth, M. D.

===

Roth, Henry J. (Joseph) 1949-
Tales From Time-Out / Henry J. Roth, Ph. D.

ISBN 10: 0-9785435-0-5
ISBN 13: 978-0-9785435-0-1

1. Humor—Fiction. 2. School Behavior—Fiction. 3. Emotional Problems—Fiction. 4. School Humor—Fiction. 5. Parents—Fiction. 6. Teachers—Fiction. I. Title

10 9 8 7 6 5 4 3 2 1

REVIEWS OF *TALES FROM TIME-OUT*

Tales From Time-Out is a must-read for any special educator or child care professional working with troubled children. Roth masterfully demonstrates how to decode children's behavior, in particular their humor, to gain understanding of the student's psychological state and how best, in crisis situations, to respond to them in an effective manner. Also, Roth does not shy away from demonstrating how even an experienced professional can be caught in the power of a youngster's emotions and sometimes make inappropriate responses.

—Robert B. Bloom, Ph.D.
Executive Director, Jewish Child & Family Services of Chicago, and Former Chairman, Department of Special Education at the College of William and Mary

===

This is a delightful, wise and important guide for parents and teachers. It is a great book and fun to read as well. The examples in this book really ring true, and help us to see how we can help children. This book is must-reading not just in helping troubled children but in helping all children at school and at home.

—Bertram J. Cohler, Ph. D.
William Rainey Harper Professor in the Social Sciences at The University of Chicago, and
Former Director of the Sonia Shankman Orthogenic School at the University of Chicago

===

This is a lovely little book, very easy to read, very enjoyable. Dr. Roth's descriptions make clear the two-fold nature of his efforts: In the discussions with the "time-outers" he helps them to develop their inner strength through increasing understanding of themselves. At the same time he does not neglect the importance of providing limits and consequences for destructive behavior. Too often people feel that the one precludes the other.

I like very much the deep respect for these "time-outers" that runs through the book. Dr. Roth's emphasis on the humor seems to be a reflection of that. These are never "bad" kids or "wise guys" whose behavior has to be reformed — they are always children who need help to master behavior that hurts both others and themselves.

I also liked the degree of involvement that a principal can have with his students and staff that this book reflects. This is a great model for leaders.

—Jacquelyn Seevak Sanders, Ph. D.
Former Director of the Sonia Shankman Orthogenic
School at the University of Chicago, and
Senior Lecturer in the Department of Education

TALES FROM TIME-OUT

$\mathcal{H}umor$ is at the heart of a loving relationship. Lorraine's illustrations extracted the meaning and essence of each tale, and brought a lively dimension to them. While looking at each illustration, I am reminded of how lucky I am to have such a funny, talented and loving wife. Finally, I hope that I have respectfully acknowledged and honored my students, from whom I have learned a great deal.

Henry Roth

January 17, 2007

TABLE of CONTENTS

STRATEGIES FOR TIME-OUT

1. Analyzing Humor
2. Effective Interpretations
3. Judgmental Comments
4. Empathic Atmosphere
5. The Excitement of Not Knowing
6. The Silent Student
7. Avoiding Anger
8. Visual vs. Verbal Techniques
9. Circular Logic
10. The Best First Questions to Ask in Time-Out
11. Questions to Ask Oneself
12. Sense of Humor

INTRODUCTION

This book contains a collection of illustrated tales, most of which originated during time-out encounters at a therapeutic day school. The school served a widely diverse population including a small special program for Orthodox Jewish students. As principal there for sixteen years, I found that students from all walks of life often reveal their emotional struggles through humorous comments.

Many of my most compelling and lasting memories involved amusing exchanges with students in time-out. These interactions illuminate how students deal with difficult situations, and the best coping strategies they have often include their sense of humor. Examining their off-the-cuff quips can help us to understand the unique ways that students ascribe meaning to their conflicted feelings. This book emphasizes the healing power of comedy.

We can do a disservice to students when we do not recognize the importance of the satire in their comments as a first draft sent from the front lines of emotional conflict. If we dismiss or minimize the value of their sarcasm, we do so at the risk of not fully appreciating their fears, beliefs and defenses. No matter how rude or disrespectful, comedy can serve as an emotional safety valve. Exploring its power to seek relief can be a worthy mission.

Finally, because this book tries to capture the intense feelings and emotions that are hidden in a funny comment, each tale selects a portion of an actual time-out encounter and compresses the event to provide a composite snapshot of the inner world of the students. In looking at the snapshot, the reader must realize that the characters and events have been fictionalized to preserve confidentiality.

FOREWORD

There is a tendency to idealize a specialized school as a place where one can take daily pride in the accomplishments of the students. Those who work at such schools know it as a complicated picture with stories of successes and failures. Humor can serve as an emotional safety valve. Without it, the students may not be as able to disguise or armor themselves against their own disturbing emotions, and even more serious acting out might occur.

No time-out situation is ever exactly like any other. Although each student in time-out handles his anger in a unique manner, all students need to have their anger mean something. So the idea of recognizing and respecting this meaning is important. We need to know "the facts" — what actually happened — and that is often embedded in symbolic form in a funny reply. When we get the facts, and the student's perception of the facts, we obtain both an individualized snapshot of the student and a universal picture of how we all ascribe meaning to our conflicted feelings.

A sarcastic comment in time-out may be triggered by an upsetting classroom event, and then becomes a means by which the student tries to restore his disturbed emotional equilibrium. Where a symptom — for example, a tic or stuttering — can be an *unconscious* response to a stressor, sarcasm is a more *conscious* response which ridicules those fears that leave the student feeling vulnerable. In short, the humorous tale is a temporary "memorial" to one's fears.

Typically, students at a therapeutic day school have a limited capacity to tolerate intense feelings and reflexively use rage or sarcasm to defend against their deep distress. Rage, anger, or sarcasm often conceals the student's underlying sadness, helplessness, or hurt at being punished, excluded, and sent to time-out. In addition, defensive rage provides a sense of temporary power and strength in a situation where the student really feels powerless. In making a joke, the student tries to balance the turbulence of his underlying distress with the equally powerful urge to deny it. The two forces coexist but are usually isolated from each other.

One place where both forces intersect is in comedy. It allows the expression of the student's conflicted feelings in a disguised form that is less anxiety-provoking. To paraphrase Freud, "Humor serves as a cooling compress to a burning wound." It helps the student to relax, comforting him so he can begin to restore his emotional equilibrium. By saying something funny, the student starts the healing process and the gaining of mastery over his personal distress from a position of strength rather than weakness.

This kind of framework for understanding these tales gives special meaning to jokes, images, and words that would otherwise be seen as superficial, insignificant, or diversionary. The tales not only reveal the student's initial disturbing reaction, but also provide a way of understanding what is happening between the student and staff at that moment. Reality has many dimensions and the concealed dimension telegraphed in these tales can be just as revealing as the exterior one we think of as "objective truth."

During time-out encounters, humor can provide important clues that can warn staff when they are caught up in feelings that hinder the therapeutic process. After all, students do not always communicate their feelings whimsically; so staff should view each playful comment as a unique opportunity to advance their understanding of the student and themselves. In this process of discovery, staff will be more likely to find and enter the student's inner world during crisis situations. In discovering the student, we find ourselves.

TALES FROM TIME-OUT

1. GREG: *Game-Boy*

Greg was in time-out for becoming verbally and physically aggressive when his teacher confronted him about stealing Monty's "Game Boy" device. In time-out, Greg denied taking the Game Boy even though the teacher saw him take it.

Once in time-out, I offered the following interpretations, to try to help him accept responsibility in a non-threatening manner:

Me: "Could it be that you wanted to show Monty, an insufferable know-it-all, that you could one-up him by stealing his Game Boy?"

Greg: "No! And I didn't steal his Game Boy!"

Me: "Despite Monty's arrogance, was it important to show that you could, in effect, 'take him down' a peg or two, by taking his Game Boy?"

Greg: "No! I told you I didn't take his Game Boy!"

Me: "When you felt ridiculed by Monty — who stole your pride, in a sense — did you want to take something special away from him in return — the Game Boy — to make up for your hurt feelings?"

Greg: "No! Like I said, I didn't take his Game Boy!"

Me: "When you feel that you've been wronged, do you perhaps tell yourself that you won't get angry, but you'll get even?"

Greg: "Okay, okay! I'll give back the Game Boy if you just please stop analyzing me. Please! You've analyzed enough! I'll do anything! Just stop already!"

Stealing was a compromise between Greg's impulse to attack and his competing need for restraint. Greg presents an example of a student who could not tolerate his own internal conflict (his rivalry with the other boy) and, as a result, he acted it out by stealing.

Why did Greg return the stolen Game Boy? I asked him that question several days after the incident, when he was more likely to give me a thoughtful response. Greg's reply:

"Dr. Roth, you seemed so sure that you knew *why* I stole the Game Boy, it was like I had no choice but to tell you, because you knew why I did it and I didn't feel like I wanted to keep lying to you anymore."

Hearing me articulate the conflict for him, Greg felt understood, and his anxiety was eased. Much of what goes on in time-out is similar to this tale. One part of the student wants to do the right thing, but he is so emotionally overwhelmed that resisting seems like the only possible alternative. A directive to a resistant student such as, "I know you did it, give it back now or you'll regret it," can be perceived as a confrontational threat. As a result, in order to restore their self-esteem and stave off feelings of powerlessness, the student either clings to his resistance, or he verbally and physically escalates the acting-out behavior.

Communicating an understanding of Greg's internal conflicts allowed him to confront the disturbing feelings that his stealing defended against. Since it was no longer necessary to deny how hurt he was inside, he was ready to disclose where he hid the Game Boy.

2. MARK: *Perks of the Job*

Mark was a ten-year-old boy, who was transferred from public school into three other therapeutic day schools, and terminated from each of them in turn. He came to our school after all three other placements did not succeed. On Mark's second day with us, he smashed a large, expensive piece of gym equipment and was sent to time-out.

Me: "You will have to repay the school for the destroyed equipment. We'll assign you a job, such as straightening up the gym equipment, and the cost of the equipment you destroyed will be deducted from your wages until it is all paid for."

Mark: "Oh, that's great! That's terrific!"

Me: "Why do you think that is terrific?"

Mark: "If you're giving me a job, that means I'm going to stay here! I don't have to worry about being kicked out again!"

Mark had spent most of his previous five school years defending himself against the hurt of his lack of connection with others. At school, he felt like an outsider and usually faulted himself for being a big disappointment; he even referred to himself as a "total loser" by the time he came to our school.

Mark's comments in time-out allowed him to embrace the splendid expectation that he would no longer be a school "transient" — now, he could invest himself in a permanent school which gave him a sense of hope for the future. The joy that Mark expressed in this tale belied the unrealistic assumption on which it rested — that his placement here would be permanent, predicated on his having a "job" here.

Nevertheless, his joy was not misguided because the tale is not really about logic; it's about Mark's fear and his wish for a meaningful connection with others.

3. CRAIG: *No Way*

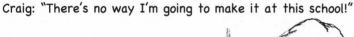

Craig, 12, was involved in a fighting incident for which he was sent to time-out. He had a number of more general issues that he needed to work on, such as self-control, being more respectful, improving his attendance, and doing more challenging academic work. While in time-out, instead of more prudently focusing on the problem at hand, I went over all of these issues with him.

Back in class, his teacher asked him, "So what did Dr. Roth tell you?"

Craig: "There's no way I'm going to make it at this school!"

Craig was not a motivated student, but he was perceptive enough to know what was required to be successful. Craig's reply to his teacher represented his lack of self-confidence, in light of my comments, which unfortunately had only served to illustrate his inadequacies. Craig's reply telegraphed his discouragement and revealed what really bothered him after seven years of school — his feeling of inevitable failure.

Weighed down by a sense of inadequacy, Craig's pattern was to turn to a trusted adult at school to rescue him from his fear of inevitable failure. The phrase "There's no way I'm going to make it at this school" reflected Craig's attempt to (a) communicate his sense of being "damaged goods" and (b) level the playing field which he perceived as stacked against him, by enlisting the teacher's support.

Angry outbursts in class concealed Craig's fragile self-esteem and enabled him to avoid his deeply embedded insecurity and see himself as strong and independent. Time-out was also used as a test to determine whether certain staff were strong enough to withstand his onslaughts, building a foundation for trust. He could then begin to verbalize his sense of being a failure.

By reciting a laundry list of Craig's school problems, I fell into the trap of confirming the failure role that Craig had ascribed to himself. A more specific approach of focusing on one problem at a time would have been more likely to help. Craig could have confronted the reality of his own limitations, and in the process, helped himself to achieve a belated mastery of his fragile self-esteem. In this manner, his expectation that someone would save him might be replaced by the expectation that he could save himself.

4. YALE:

Pretending

Yale was 12 years old and had an explosive relationship with an abusive father. When I came to see him in time-out, he was hitting himself in the face.

Me: "Why are you hitting yourself?" I asked, taking his hands away.

Yale: "I'm pretending that I'm my father, so I can be the one to beat the hell out of me!"

A Matter of Luck

Again in time-out, I was comparing Yale's problems with his teacher to his current conflicts with his Dad. They had had an intense argument just before school started. I tried to encourage Yale that once he was able to overcome his father-son conflict, the problems with his teacher would be less overwhelming.

Me: "Could it be that some part of you may be wanting your teacher to fail you in the same way that you feel your father has failed you?"

Yale: "Dr. Roth, I want you to know that just because I don't understand a word you're saying doesn't mean you are a bad principal."

Me: "It sounds like you're thinking that I'm not connecting with what you really feel."

Yale: "Anything you tell me that relates to what I really feel is just a matter of luck."

Yale was twelve years old and lived with his father in a single-parent home. Before this time-out encounter, Yale had not been able to convey the anxiety and distress he experienced with his father. No one had been able to bear witness to the reality of this conflicted and painful relationship. As a result, Yale disavowed his pain and any hope of communicating it, and focused instead on making trouble in class. He diverted his attention because he was convinced that there was no hope of relief from his suffering and isolation. The comments in time-out represent Yale's attempt to process this upsetting relationship with his father at a more conscious level of understanding.

Yale would often argue with his father just before leaving for school. In the first part of this tale, what takes place is the role reversal of Yale's father as the child and Yale as the father. Then, Yale repeats the demeaning things his father would say to him before he left for school. At home, Yale feared his vulnerability; but in the time-out tale, his own role-playing reversal created a sense of empowerment, filling in the desperation at Yale's core with bursts of energy and resolve.

This time-out tale illustrates how Yale used an alternative means of expressing his conflicted feelings, and the complexity of his emotional turbulence. It became a first step for future discussions that could lead to therapeutic progress. Interestingly, Yale enjoyed reading Bible stories, and his favorite story from the Bible involved Samson bringing down the Philistines in a way that also brought about Samson's own death — another manifestation of an effort to hurt others in spite of also hurting oneself.

In the second part of this tale, which occurred six months later, Yale communicated some of the difficulties he was having with his father in a manner that is more natural for an adolescent, through wit and sarcasm. An argument before school had left Yale hurt and he needed to protect himself. My attempts to enhance his self-awareness were premature. Yale was not ready to betray his father by talking with me about their conflicts in a straightforward manner; instead Yale deflected the issue by putting me down in a joking manner. Through sarcasm, he discharged some of the hostile feelings he had for his father, as a result of their early morning argument, and generally as a result of their ongoing conflicts.

A "transitional object" is something — a blanket or a doll, for example — to which a child attaches feelings he has for a significant other, in order to avoid separation anxiety. In this time-out tale, Yale uses me as if I were a transitional object for his father. In so doing, he obtains some of the satisfaction that he would have received if he had put down his father (symbolized by me) during their troublesome interaction before school. The hostility Yale projected onto me (in the form of a sarcastic interaction) allowed him to reassure himself that he was in control.

Besides being another example of how students are capable of communicating their compelling feelings through humor, this tale illustrates how Yale continued to process his relationship with his father at a progressively healthier level of adjustment.

When Yale graduated from high school I knew I would miss him. His ability to use sarcasm to make me laugh and to see my shortcomings helped me to negotiate more effectively the challenges of time-out with other students.

5. PHIL: *Talk to Yourself*

Phil, a 14-year-old boy, was sent to time-out due to a temper outburst he had. The teacher had not allowed him to use the computer until he finished his other assignments.

In time-out, I tried to talk Phil down from his anger by explaining that his anger-outburst was out of line with what the teacher did.

Me: "You can try reminding yourself how much the teacher helped you throughout the school year. You can work out your anger by using this kind of 'self talk'."

Phil: "If you expect me to talk myself out of being angry, then I expect you to talk yourself out of keeping me in time-out!"

In the encounter with Phil, I was operating under two assumptions: First, the student can rethink himself out of the problem; and second, by giving the student a more realistic perspective of the situation he is bound to act in a more appropriate manner.

Phil's response suggested that for him the important factor was not his unrealistic perspective but the anger he felt at not getting his own way. Phil is saying that the task of changing his behavior lies in talking to him about his anger, rather than in talking him out of it. Did I really believe that I would change my own behavior if the situation were reversed?

There is a delicate balance in confronting individual students with their overreactions. Too little confrontation produces minimal opportunities for change and too much confrontation produces maximum opportunities for opposition.

In this tale, Phil attempts to expose my expectation as absurd, in order to free himself from the obligation to fulfill it. His humorous response gave him momentary relief from the pressure of a perceived unrealistic expectation, and reduced his anxiety about the seriousness of his anger problem. His message was, "Nothing you say about me changing myself really matters because you can't change yourself any better than I can!" Hence, his right to be angry.

6. ABE: *In the First Place*

Abe was in time-out for misbehaving in class. I asked him if he used the 4-step pre-arranged "STAR" plan he had worked on with his therapist, to avoid having to go to time-out in the future:

1. <u>S</u>top and count to 10
2. <u>T</u>hink about the problem
3. <u>A</u>ssess the options
4. <u>R</u>espond based on #3

Abe: "If I could remember everything in that plan, I wouldn't be in time-out in the first place."

Abe was 15 years old, and his history included physical aggression toward others, plus alcohol and drug abuse. From the beginning of any encounter, Abe targeted staff as the "enemy." His demanding and aggressive behavior could evoke strong negative feelings from others. He was often hostile and inappropriate with his sarcasm. Sometimes his offensiveness invited anger, which he then found insulting, and he reacted with physical aggression. In this tale, Abe's comeback was harmless, and allowed him to communicate his anger without being offensive.

Of course, it is important to teach students to think about and examine their options before they respond to a provocative situation. However, for Abe, his humor served as a red flag that a different kind of de-escalating strategy should be used, more "feeling-based" than "thinking-based." In joking, Abe attempted to free himself from following the plan by viewing it as an absurdity. He was telling me that I was so invested in the "plan" that I did not have a clue about what it was like to be out of control. And, if I didn't have a clue, how could I expect Abe to control himself?

Abe did not always have rational control at his disposal. He acted on impulse and on his strong emotions. Using one perspective such as the "STAR" strategy for all students may end up working against a particular student's best interests.

7. LON: *Friends Like These*

Lon, a 15-year-old boy, was sent to time-out for fighting with Mike, another student in his class.

Me: "Why did you start fighting with Mike?"

Lon: "I hate Mike, he's terrible. He's not even loyal to his girlfriend. He cheats on her. He plays around with other girls and lies about it. He would even stab his own mother in the back. I know he's stolen money from her and then used it to buy lunch."

Me: "Where did you get this information?"
Lon: "From Mike. He's my best friend."

Lon's mother was a severe alcoholic, and he had devoted his early years to worrying about her and caring for her physical and emotional health. Even as a young child, Lon would be looking for his mother at the local bars. From the time he entered our school at age ten, Lon wanted to recapture what he felt robbed of — the security of someone taking care of him — and what he now felt entitled to.

In school, his sense of being robbed or victimized showed itself in his intense competition with his peers, who he imagined were living out what he missed. Lon frequently viewed staff as objects to meet his needs. Out in the community, he had also succumbed to using alcohol and drugs himself.

At home, Lon had developed a hostile-dependent relationship with his mother that alternated between love and hate. When he perceived her as being too close, which was often, because he felt emotionally over-obligated to her, he feared that he would lose his "macho" identity. At that point, he would distance himself from her by demeaning her character. Then, feeling both lonely and guilty, he verbalized physical complaints in order to solicit a nurturing response from her and regain the comfort of a close maternal relationship.

In this time-out tale, we see how Lon's feelings toward Mike mirrored the conflicted relationship he had with his mother — anger at their actions, but enduring bonds. It proved helpful to provide Lon with a feeling of being cared for, protected and understood. It was counterproductive to challenge him to rethink his heightened sense of victimization; this only led to a cycle of hurt, escalating anger, and physical acting-out. A strategy of being emotionally supportive communicated compassion to Lon, and encouraged him to return to class without clinging to a sense of being cheated by staff, students, or circumstances.

8. LAURA: *A Momentary Wish*

Laura is a 14-year-old girl who tended to be very emotional and self-involved. During one episode in time-out, I noticed that she was breathing harder, talking at a faster pace, and her tone was more frenetic than usual.

Me: "Are you okay?"

Laura: "Sure I'm fine. It was just a momentary wish that I could do well at school. I'm sure it'll pass."

Fashion Statement

Laura also had a keen eye for fashion — or lack thereof. I can always count on her for an insightful and clever critique. Once when my shirt and tie were especially less than well-coordinated, Laura wanted to let me know that. At the same time, she apparently wanted to soften the blow to my ego. Passing me in the hallway, she proclaimed, "Now there's a bold choice of colors!"

In school, Laura was intolerant of being on the receiving end of a relationship, a position that made her feel less in control and more vulnerable. Laura did not feel worthy enough to receive unless she gave something of herself first. In her relationships with males, Laura often experienced disappointment, failure, rejection, and physical abuse. She found it hard to leave these abusive relationships, in spite of the emotional and physical pain she endured.

In part, her quick wit and sophisticated repartee gave her hope that she had something powerful in her bag of tricks that would make others appreciate and value her as an individual. In particular, in dealing with males, she hoped that her wit would move men to appreciate her as she wanted to be appreciated by a rejecting and distant father. Ultimately, by making people laugh, Laura hoped that she would find the man of her dreams.

"Now there's a bold choice of colors," reflected Laura's need to be critical of others (who might represent her father) and do it in an entertaining manner. Desperate to find reassurance from an accepting male, she used amusing banter to attract men and, at the same time, to keep them at a distance, to defend against her fear of rejection.

As Freud warned, "We are never so defenseless against suffering as when we love; never as helplessly unhappy as when we have lost our loved object or its love." In part, Laura used her highly developed sense of comic style to prevent meaningful communication between herself and others.

In working with Laura, it was important to respect and not be offended by her sarcasm. The goal was to help her see that satire used in a positive manner — allowing others to experience her creativity, warmth, and the unique way that she defined herself — could help her to form healthy relationships.

After she graduated from high school, Laura often came back to visit with the staff. On one occasion she mentioned to me that she was reading a psychology book and found an article about earliest childhood recollections (ECR's). She proceeded to tell me her ECR and then asked, "I want to know if you think that's what really happened or if I colored it so I have an excuse to keep the guys as far away as possible from me." Such questions give meaning and a sense of purpose to the mission of the school.

9. SAMUEL: *Fashion Non-Statement*

Samuel was a 14-year-old Jewish boy in a counseling group I led with the Orthodox high school class. One of the more persistent themes is that they need to follow all of the rules and regulations that are part of their Jewish Orthodoxy, in addition to the other more generic rules and regulations of school, and of life in general.

Samuel: "As a Jewish Principal of a school, and leading an Orthodox counseling group, why do you not wear a *kippah* (*yarmulke*, or skull cap)?"

Me: "Since we have many non-Jewish students in the school, with many African-Americans and Latinos, I try to represent the whole school, not just the Jewish students."

Samuel: "Well, then why don't you wear baggy pants and an earring?"

Samuel had not yet mastered his own conflicted feelings regarding his duty to religion versus his duty to himself. As a result, he found it amusing to tease me about the same type of issues. Samuel transformed his mixed feelings about connecting with the religious and secular world into a humorous critique of my conflicted school allegiances.

As is the case for most sarcasm, the person being ridiculed represents much of what the teller repudiates in himself. Samuel occasionally enjoyed repeating this tale, perhaps because it symbolized his triumph in getting rid of his own conflicted religious feelings. If Samuel had been aware of some of the underlying dynamics embedded in this tale, it probably would have lost its appeal.

Over time, Samuel was able to see how this tale connected to important issues in his life, and provided clues about how to address them. As Samuel matured, he changed the way he looked at the tale to fit his evolving and more sophisticated understanding of himself. The tale served as a historical "tunnel" through which Samuel could be taken back to his conflicted religious feelings and forward to how he used levity to eschew these feelings by making light of them.

As Mark Twain said, "The secret source of humor is not joy, but sorrow...Perhaps laughter is just a less painful kind of tears."

10. MICKEY: *Dr. Evil*

Mickey was in time-out and kept referring to me as "The Evil Dr. Roth."

Me: "Mickey, when you stop calling me 'The Evil Dr. Roth' and give me five quiet minutes, then we can discuss what happened and you can go back to class. But, the five minutes do not start until you stop referring to me as 'The Evil Dr. Roth.'"

Mickey: "Okay, then — I'll just call you 'Dr. E.'"

In this tale, Mickey had been processing the fact that the previous day I had talked to him and his parents about returning part-time to public school ("mainstreaming"). Instead of hearing my comments as well-earned recognition, Mickey was sure that the school was tired of him, and — I in particular — just wanted to kick him out. By calling me "Dr. E," Mickey saw himself as a "warrior" doing battle against a malevolent or uncaring principal. Mickey's perception at the time was clear, even if it were tempered by a clever comment. In addition, Mickey was feeling vulnerable about leaving the school and his sarcasm concealed a strong fear of rejection.

In time-out, if Mickey's sarcasm had been confronted as rude or inappropriate, it would have closed off the opportunity to understand the meaning behind it. It was as though Mickey were saying, "Humor is my best effort to relax myself and restore my emotional balance which has been shaken by your rejection of me. If you get angry at me for my 'Dr. E' joke, I'll be left with nothing and I'll act out even more." When Mickey and I actually talked, after a five-minute "chill-out," he was able to see that calling me "The Evil Dr. Roth" was a reaction to feeling rejected by me and his fear and uncertainty about returning to public school.

Maybe I was too quick to tell Mickey to stop referring to me as the "evil Dr. Roth." In my idealized self-image, I want to see myself as calm and assured in the middle of a crisis. Over time, it's easy to start thinking, "You know, that's right — I *am* the good Dr. Roth," but that's not conducive to learning and growing as a professional. To handle a crisis is to risk tarnishing one's idealized self-image. Thus, when Mickey calls me "Dr. E" it is important to listen for the hidden message embedded in the "sting" and to use this message to plan the most helpful move.

11. SIMCHA: *All You Need to Know*

Simcha was a 14-year old Orthodox Jewish boy who had been at our school for several years. His misbehavior frequently landed him in time-out. During one of these occasions, after he had calmed down enough, I told him that his misbehavior at times is a "gift" to the class — a way to win the approval of the other boys in his class.

"Well," he responded, "I wasn't aware that I was using my misbehavior as giving a gift to the other children."

I said, "That's the whole purpose of this school — to help you think about what you are doing before you act."

Simcha thought about that and then said, "Well, I wish you had told me that three years ago when I got here. If that's all I need to know, I can pack my things right now and leave!"

Simcha's overall conflict involved struggling with the desire for recognition and his denial of that need. At school, Simcha's security rested on the approval he received from his peers, negative or positive, and his fear of not obtaining that approval. In part, Simcha's insecurity was based on his belief that no matter how hard he tried, his best was never going to be good enough for his peers. Moreover, he wanted to be accepted by his peers and at the same time he resented his dependency on them.

In part, Simcha used misbehavior to win peer-approval in order to bury deeply embedded feelings of insecurity. He offered his misbehavior as a "gift" to the other students. In one case, a teacher had given Simcha's friend several warnings for disobeying a rule. After the third warning, Simcha feared that his friend might be punished. He then diverted the teacher's attention by throwing his *yarmulke* (skullcap) at him. Simcha was aware of a class rule which held that throwing things at others resulted in an automatic time-out. At that point, the teacher focused his attention on Simcha, rather than his friend, and sent him to time-out. That was a "gift" to his friend.

Being ignored triggered Simcha's insecurity that he was no longer the gift-bearing student he fashioned himself to be. The goal for Simcha was to find meaning and security within himself, without "bearing gifts" to accomplish that.

12. WILLIAM: *Millionaire*

William was sent to time-out for refusing to do his work, then becoming verbally abusive toward the teacher and being asked to leave the room. Finally he somehow flung himself onto the teacher's desk as if to threaten her. She called for the crisis teacher, who escorted William to time-out. I got there shortly afterward, but neither of us could get a clear picture from William of what had actually happened. He was too anxious, angry, and talking rapidly.

In an effort to get a better handle on the situation, I asked William to answer the following questions:

Me: "Question Number One: Did you tell the teacher that the work was too hard, or did you tell her that you had no intention of doing any work at all?"

William: "Too hard."

Me: "Question Number Two: Did you refuse to leave the classroom after being asked?"

William: "No"

Me: "Question Number Three: Did you throw yourself at the teacher's desk, or did you trip and fall onto it?"

William: "I tripped and fell."

Me: "Okay, your answers have been quick and to-the-point. So far, so good."

William: "I wish you were Regis Philbin. By now I'd be a millionaire!"

William was nine years old and typically resisted acknowledging or exploring the reasons that he was sent to time-out. During time-out encounters, he would look at me with skepticism — alert but scornful. The very act of being excluded from the classroom left him feeling misunderstood and violated. His feelings were too strongly defended against to be accessible through a literal reconstruction of what happened. In part, William denied his physically aggressive behavior because it was disturbing to him, and caused him to feel anxious and stressed, in light of his own history of physical abuse.

William's response indicated that he might have believed that I was more likely to help him if I were a game show host than an interrogating principal. He was probably right. Locked into a logical sequence of events, I gave myself little leeway to uncover William's perception of what happened and understand the sequence of his thoughts and feelings that were mirrored in the conflict. My preoccupation with the "Just the facts, kid," jeopardized my getting to the heart of the matter. Of course, there are many benefits to asking close-ended questions. However, for William, asking such questions could be counterproductive because it telegraphed to him that the staff person did not try to view what had happened from his perspective.

Controlling the discussion is one thing; controlling oneself is another. Sometimes in an effort to resolve a crisis quickly — hence "showcasing" one's therapeutic skills — we are prone to the same vanities and compulsions that challenge the students. To recognize these forces is to acknowledge how vulnerable we all are in the grip of anxiety-provoking crises.

13. TOMMY: *Hold the Questions*

Tommy was a 12-year-old boy who was frequently counseled in time-out about appropriate and inappropriate behavior in the classroom. At one point I came to time-out when Tommy was there.

By the time I arrived, he had already calmed down somewhat, and was eager to get back to class.

Me: "Hello, Tommy, I..."

Tommy: "Doc! Just give me the punishment! I'll give you my thoughts and feelings later!"

Whenever I meet with students in time-out, I first try to calm them down. Then, when they are more composed, I ask questions and try to get them to talk about what happened and why; and we discuss their thoughts and feelings about what happened. After that is clarified, we agree on some appropriate consequences for the misbehavior. That may be loss of gym time or computer privileges, or whatever is consistent with their misbehavior that resulted in the time-out.

In class, Tommy incited angry or rejecting responses from others — he often made fun of both staff and other students. These would result in angry counterattacks, which then made him feel victimized. In addition, he seemed repelled by people who consistently tried to treat him well or show understanding.

In this tale, Tommy says that he would prefer to hear his punishment right away, without disclosing his thoughts and feelings. In response, I told him, "It would be difficult to decide what to do when I haven't heard 'your side' of the story."

At that point, Tommy recalled a conversation we had in time-out more than six months earlier. Tommy recalled my observation that he appeared to get angry with me even when I was patient and respectful with him. Now, six months later, Tommy said that maybe he wanted me to be stricter, tougher, so I could control his bad behavior for him. He then revealed to me that his father, a violent man, was in jail (unbeknownst to Tommy, this information had been available to me when we first took him into the school).

I told Tommy that, given what he had just told me, he had very good reasons not to share himself with others. It was easier for him to deal with adults who were not nice to him, like his father, because he could fight back and keep them at a distance.

In summary, Tommy had constructed a false-self which was sarcastic, defensive, and attacking. His false-self was designed to protect his true-self from being exploited ever again by uncaring, disrespectful, or abusive adults. The very idea of disclosing his thoughts and feelings made Tommy feel vulnerable, dependent, and full of rage for everything that happened to him. It would take a commitment from Tommy to gain insight into how he distanced himself from others; and a great deal more time before Tommy would be able to face the devastating implications of his rage toward his father.

14. DANIEL & CHAIM: *The Messiah*

Daniel and Chaim were 16-year-old Orthodox Jewish boys who tended to be very self-absorbed and grandiose. They became agitated with each other one day and were unable to be settled back down. That necessitated both of them being taken to time-out, separately.

Once in time-out, I learned that Daniel had become upset during a group therapy session, when he and Chaim had the following exchange:

Chaim: "You talk like you think you are the Messiah [Savior]."

Daniel: "That's right! And you're just jealous because you're not the Messiah!" And so began the fight.

Chaim, when confronted with a peer whose conflicts mirrored his own, ridiculed and exaggerated the other student's problems. Name-calling and sarcasm became a way to defend against disturbing aspects of himself. In this tale, not only did Daniel and Chaim disown their own disturbing problems, but they attributed them to each other. Moreover, their sarcasm carried a religious spin, making the encounter even more emotionally charged.

In time-out, I tried to avoid entanglement in the religious overtones of the sarcasm. Chaim had his pride tied up in attributing his own shortcomings to Daniel. It was important to create opportunities for him to explore his feelings regarding their relationship. For example, by asking Chaim, "Don't you get tired of trying to prove that Daniel is really at fault?" one reveals an appreciation of Chaim's need to avoid facing his own failings in a direct manner. This helped Chaim experience his time-out encounter from a position of safety in which potentially explosive emotions were contained, rather than escalated.

Daniel's grandiose manner proved to him how important he was; otherwise why would Chaim be so threatened by him? Daniel had excuses for everything — the fault was always outside himself. He wanted others to think he was perfect to compensate for his self-doubt. His self-doubt was so deep-seated that he automatically withdrew behind a mask of superiority whenever he experienced internal conflict or encountered disagreements.

In time-out, Daniel was more likely to view me as non-threatening and cooperative if I didn't challenge or contradict him. It was more useful to ask Daniel for advice versus information. For example, I might ask him, "If you were the principal, what would you do in a situation like this?" Asking for information from Daniel was potentially threatening, whereas he viewed giving advice as less offensive.

15. HARVEY: *No Reason at All*

Our two time-out rooms were, unfortunately, right next to each other. Harvey, age 15, in one time-out room, heard the sound of Jack yelling and screaming in the adjacent time-out room.

Harvey: "Poor kid! You people are cruel! I'm sure Jack didn't do anything so bad that he had to be sent to time-out! I should report you all to D.C.F.S [Department of Children and Family Services]!"

Me: "Are you thinking that you have been treated unfairly by being sent to time-out?"

Harvey: "Me?! Treated unfairly? Just because I was sent to time-out for no other reason than that the teacher hates me? Is that any reason to think that Jack is crying for no reason, too? Do you think I'm crazy?!"

To survive his difficult childhood, Harvey tried his best to put his traumatic experiences behind him. He had been placed in no fewer than ten foster homes since he was nine years old. Harvey was faced with two opposing forces: One, his desire for a better life; and two, his promise to himself that he would never forget his intense suffering, that is, moving from one foster placement to another. Accordingly, Harvey felt emotionally obligated to be loyal to other suffering students and help them through their personal misery by being a witness to their pain and a champion for their cause.

The encoded message in Harvey's tale is, "I will never forget where I came from because I'm committed to fighting battles for vulnerable and victimized students." These battles are a memorial to his traumatic past and confer a special meaning and purpose to the wounded child he was and to the wounded teenager he became. Harvey grabs onto the role of "protector," afraid to let go. Letting go would mean abandoning his past and leaving his pain behind. However, holding onto his past is painful. He finds temporary relief from the discomfort through cathartic outbursts that bring out the message of his own disturbing past.

In this tale, Harvey finds a clear and moving symbol in the student in the neighboring time-out room, for his conflicted feelings about his unfortunate and chaotic childhood experiences.

16. JAKE: *The Answer*

Jake was in time-out, and when I got there, I asked my usual question: "What happened?"

Jake: "The teacher wanted me to go to time-out."

Me: "What did you do?"

Jake: "I didn't do anything! I told you, he just wanted me to go to time-out. He doesn't like me."

Me: "How do you know he doesn't like you?"

Jake: "I'm in time-out, so there's your answer."

Like many other students at the school who internalize their problems, Jake was a non-demonstrative person; in fact, he was painfully uncomfortable around new people or facing an unfamiliar situation. In time-out I tried to pursue a gentle esteem-building approach to help strengthen his self-confidence before exploring other problems. For example, I highlighted Jake's strengths and accomplishments before identifying the problematic circumstances that led to the time-out.

Jake also responded well to a particular crisis worker who was much less supportive of him and sometimes abrupt and judgmental. What was the motivation for a shy student such as Jake to identify with someone who presented himself so differently? Perhaps Jake recognized that people who externalize their stress have something useful to say to those who internalize it; and that a more assertive style, depending on the circumstances, can be a useful, productive way to interact with others.

Before we make value judgments about what works in time-out we need to consider that a diverse staff and competing strategies are important aspects of a student's therapeutic education. Fundamental differences in the way staff approached Jake helped him to integrate the notion that there were staff who were competent and helpful and still were different from himself.

17. KIRK: *Five Quiet Minutes*

Kirk was sent to time-out for hitting his teacher. He did not hurt the teacher, as the punch was more for show than for injury. In time-out, Kirk offered to apologize to the teacher. That was okay, but before he apologized, he had to first give me five "quiet minutes." The ability to be quiet for five minutes was necessary to ascertain the student's readiness to go back to class.

Kirk: "Okay, I'm ready to say I'm sorry now."

Me: "Great, I'm glad to hear that. But you still have to give me five quiet minutes before you can go back to class.

Kirk: "No, I want to say I'm sorry *now.*"

Me: "Why do you need to say you are sorry now? I'm sure it can wait five minutes, and then you will be ready to go back to class."

Kirk: "No, I need to say it now. If I'm going to lie, I want to get it over with quickly!"

Kirk, a gifted, underachieving student, was raised in a group home and had never seen his parents. Kirk felt entitled to having our staff make up the difference to him and provide emotional support and nurturance that he never received from parents. Kirk described himself as a "deal-maker" and constantly engaged staff to buy things for him such as food, soft drinks, or other gifts. After negotiating with Kirk, one felt that the underlying challenge he posed was "How much can I get from you before you give up on me?"

If Kirk failed to obtain his demands, he became more defiant, reenacting his rage over his sense of abandonment by his parents. It was impossible to provide Kirk with what he longed for — a relationship with someone who could fill that emotional void. Kirk could not let anyone become important to him for fear that they, too, would eventually abandon him. Hence, Kirk was willing to give the staff what they wanted — an apology — while at the same time telling them it would be no more than "lip service." His manipulative and demanding mannerisms served in part to keep others at a safe distance.

18. LARRY: *The Warrior*

Larry, an 11-year-old boy, was convinced that one of his peers was the teacher's pet. As a result, Larry became aggressive with the other student and was eventually taken to time-out. When I arrived in time-out, I could see that Larry did not seem particularly upset, and even appeared to be happy. I asked him, "Is it possible that you are enjoying this time-out?"

Larry: "Yes"

Me: "And why is that?"

Larry (smiling): "It's better to be a warrior in here than a wimpy teacher's pet in class!"

As a parent might compensate for neglecting his child by indulging him with gifts, so Larry indulged his self-image as a warrior in order to compensate for his low self-esteem. Being sent to time-out communicated his need to be seen as a hero, a champion, and a warrior for the cause.

Larry saw in the "teacher's pet" a caricature of what he found unappealing in himself, that is, the obligation to impress others. In addition, the "teacher's pet" symbolized a compliant attitude that he found threatening. Larry discharged his anxiety by projecting it onto the teacher's pet and presented himself in a way that made him look strong.

Interestingly, on occasion, the teacher's pet provoked Larry and had to be sent to time-out himself. Each used the other as a foil to seek a strength that he lacked in himself.

19. MARY: *Really Smart*

Mary's mother came to the school for a conference. The three of us met in my office. Mary sat looking around the room, as though she couldn't care less about the conference.

Mother: "Mary, you should pay attention to Dr. Roth!"

Mary: "Why should I?"

Mother: "He's very smart! He even teaches college courses at Northeastern University."

Mary: "Oh, really? Well, if he were really smart, he'd be teaching at Harvard."

Send In a Woman

Mary had become aggressive in class and was taken to time-out. I came in and helped to calm her down a bit, and then I was going to leave her with the crisis worker who had brought her to time-out.

Mary: "I don't want to be in here alone with a man!"

Although the male crisis worker was very professional and non-threatening, we agreed to Mary's request, and called Sophie, who was available. Sophie was very caring and compassionate, popular with students and staff alike. Sophie preferred a rather tailored style of dress, slacks and blazers.

When Sophie came into the time-out room, Mary proclaimed unabashedly, "Hey! I asked you to send in a woman, not a wannabe!"

Making Room

Mary made fun of a heavy-set boy in physical education class for trying to exercise. When the teacher asked her to stop deriding the boy, her verbal intimidation escalated even more and finally she was sent to time-out.

Me: "Mary, can you explain why you insisted on verbally abusing the boy, given that at least he was trying to lose weight by exercising?"

Mary: "I don't think he was trying to lose weight. I think he was just making room for more dinner!"

Mary's hostility was severe. It derived, in part, from her identification with a hostile and attacking father and several equally traumatic experiences with staff from the four different schools she had attended before coming to ours. At one school, a teacher had been convicted in court of physically attacking her.

Mary's strong need to evoke a negative response in others made it difficult for staff to maintain a therapeutic and supportive attitude toward her. Mary re-enacted with staff the trauma of her relationship with her father and then used their negative reactions to justify her hostile aggression. Basically, her sarcasm was one way to take away the staffs' power to intimidate her. Comedian Lenny Bruce said, "Satire is tragedy-plus-time."

Mary used hurtful words because she was hurting inside and wanted others to hurt, too. Too little time since her severe traumas had passed for Mary to distance herself from her pain and find comfort in anything less than destructive sarcasm. It would take more time and staff who were willing to demonstrate an accepting manner, even if they were put off by Mary's values and views. Unfortunately, this is not always possible. It is much easier to demonstrate positive regard when a student flatters a teacher's self-image or seems to be under their control. A student like Mary who demeans others reminds us of our responsibility to be respectful and professional, no matter what the circumstances.

In time-out we are shaped as much by our encounters with difficult students, such as Mary, as with the students who are not as attacking and hostile. It is important not to become the person with the clever comeback line that deflates students' grandiosity. We must remain respectful of Mary, even if she tries to turn our professional credentials against us or demeans another staff person or student. Professionally, one can benefit as much by being the target of Mary's ire as from students who idealize or respect our authority.

20. ALI: *Paranoid*

Ali was in time-out when I arrived and asked him what happened.

Ali: "My teacher is paranoid!"

Me: "Tell me what you mean by that?"

Ali: "Pa-ra-noid means "Beyond annoyed" as in "Para-psychology!"

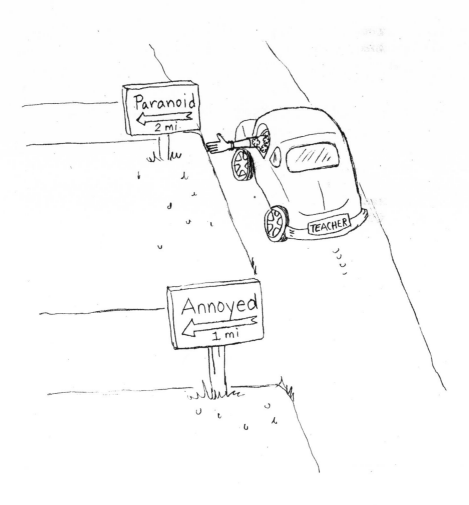

Ali, a bright 14-year-old boy of Arab origin, had been in this country for only a few years, but had obtained an excellent command of English. He understood the actual meaning of the word "paranoid." He used it in a pun of sorts to express his feelings that his teacher was "annoyed" with him, and that everyone in the school — despite its focus on "psychology" as well as education — was "against" him. He exaggerated the teacher's annoyance to justify his anxiety about feeling like an outsider. Ali's spontaneous conviction that everyone was "out to get him" was difficult to overcome.

In this tale, the encoded message is, "My teacher is annoyed with me because she has expectations of me which are beyond what she expects from other, non-Arab, students." Ali brought attention to his underlying feelings — the sense of being discriminated against as an outsider — and he hoped to obtain acknowledgment and validation for this perception in time-out. In short, Ali projected his annoyance and anxiety about being considered a threat because he was Arab onto the teacher: "I'm not annoyed, my teacher is; I'm not paranoid, my teacher is."

21. KENTON: *Accepting Diversity, Part I*

Kenton was 8 years old when he came to our school. His mother was deceased and his father was not in the picture at all. During his first Christmas with us, Kenton's second-grade class went on a field trip to the mall to see Santa. When it was Kenton's turn, he told Santa that he wanted his mother back. "Santa" said that he couldn't do that, but would listen to anything else Kenton wanted to request. Kenton began to punch and kick Santa and pull his beard. He was brought back to school and was taken into time-out because he was still agitated and yelling.

In time-out, I asked Kenton what had happened. He said, "I asked Santa to bring my Mommy back, and he said he couldn't do it." Then he began to cry, "I want my Mommy, I want my Mommy..."

I said, as gently as I could, "But you still have the gift of memories of your mother... Santa cannot give you any better gift than that."

Kenton exploded at me, "You f---ing Jew! You don't know s--- about Santa Claus!"

22. ETAN: *Accepting Diversity, Part II*

Etan, an 11-year-old Orthodox Jewish boy, had been sent to time-out, and I came in to see if I could find out what had happened, and possibly help.

Me: "So what brought you to time-out today?"

Etan: "Teacher sent me because she said I was acting like an Indian!"

Me: "What do you mean?"

Etan: "I was acting like an Indian so she sent me to time-out!"

Me: "How were you acting like an Indian?"

Etan: "You know! You know! 'Like an Indian!' That's what she said!"

Etan seemed unable to give me a description of exactly what he was doing that resulted in his being sent to time-out. I tapped my mouth in the "whoop-whoop" manner that children do to imitate a Native American war cry.

Me: "Is *this* what you were doing? Like Cowboys-and-Indians?"

Etan: "No, no, no," he answered, disgustedly. "Not *that* kind of Indian! A *Dunkin' Donuts* Indian!"

23. OLIVER: *Accepting Diversity, Part III*

Oliver was 14 years old, completely out of control, and sent to time-out. When I arrived at time-out, he immediately began cursing at me, calling me a bald, Jewish bastard.

Me: "I don't like being called names like that."

Oliver: "Then you shouldn't have become principal of this school!"

Me: "Why do you think I wanted to be principal of this school?"

Oliver: "Because you want everyone to respect you. I want to make sure that doesn't happen!"

One senses that everything these students hear, feel, or see is immediately verbalized without inhibition and with total disregard as to what is appropriate language during a conversation with adults. Some may be offended by the blatant racist, ethnic, and religious slurs contained in these three tales. But the issue is not whether these comments should be tolerated — clearly, they are unacceptable — the issue here is *intention*.

These comments were made by children in crisis. The purpose is not to humiliate a marginalized group, or to be irreverent. The purpose is to restore one's emotional equilibrium, which has been shaken by a crisis. As a result, the students discharge their threatened feelings onto a foreign source. The slurs are less disturbing to them than facing their threatened feelings. In this manner, their ideal self-image can gradually reemerge, despite the emotional turbulence caused by the time-out encounter.

At some point the students will need to learn that marginalized groups are not responsible for their threatened feelings, and that using slurs will not effectively restore their self-esteem. Eventually, these students will have to face the roots of their own inadequacies. One effective way to prevent slurs is to hold ourselves up as an example of how to treat others with dignity and respect when we are attacked. Indeed, we are ethically and professionally obligated to set an example that we want the students to follow at school, when they feel attacked by other students or by staff.

Clinically, uninhibited and derogatory language can be used to develop a better understanding of that portion of our own presentation that touches something passionate inside the student. For example, in the case of Kenton, his knowledge of my background and our ongoing relationship represented many of his internalized family conflicts. These conflicts may have been consciously forgotten, but always active and easily triggered during stressful situations such as time-out. In time-out, internal conflicts are often expressed directly enough for staff to recognize them, if they are not put off by the inappropriate language. Without the accompanying slur/swear words, one would be unable to observe how the intensity of their internal distress is proportional to the intensity of their word selection.

24. MANNY: *Impatient*

Manny became impatient waiting for his teacher's help. He had a temper outburst, disrupted the class, and was sent to time-out. I had been talking with another child in time-out, but went to see Manny as soon as I could get away.

Manny: "Are you trying to help me or make things worse?"

Me: "Why, help, of course! How could I make things worse?"

Manny: "I had to wait longer to see *you* than I did for my teacher!"

Me: "Well, I'm sorry for the delay, but let's see if we can come to a meeting of the minds."

Manny: "If we're going to have a meeting of the minds, you're going to have to be on time!"

Manny was diagnosed with Attention Deficit Hyperactivity Disorder (ADHD), and presented himself at school in a distractible and unfocused manner. At home, Manny felt that he was under constant pressure to get outstanding grades, and he developed the belief that he could never live up to the high expectations of his parents. To relieve his discouragement, and the guilt feelings it aroused, Manny used humor to laugh at the things that scared him. He mocked and ridiculed others who failed to meet his own expectations, and that was one way to defend himself against his disappointment in himself.

This time-out tale illustrates how Manny uses humor to express his impatience safely, without having to acknowledge the role that he played in creating the problem itself. The basic question with Manny was the extent to which the staff should accommodate his impatience. Clearly, staff should not reinforce Manny's unrealistic expectation of receiving immediate gratification. The goal should be to transform his need for immediate gratification into the capacity to tolerate reasonable frustration.

On the other hand, what is a reasonable waiting time for an impatient student? If staff adjusts by shortening the waiting time for Manny, he is afforded short-term relief; but there is no long-term resolution to the problem. If the waiting time for Manny is kept the same as it is for everyone else, we run the risk of not providing him with an individualized behavior program that meets his specific needs. The potential reward for developing an individualized program for Manny most likely exceeds the potential drawbacks.

25. RONNIE: *Empathy*

Ronnie was ten years old and was referred to our school for hitting himself when he felt too stressed by circumstances. As a result of losing control at school, he often found himself in time-out, due to the disruptive effect this behavior had on the class, as well as for his own safety.

On one occasion, while in time-out with his teacher's aide, he drew a picture on the wall of Jesus on the Cross. The aide allowed him to do it, because at least Ronnie had stopped screaming and hitting himself.

When I came into time-out to talk to him, I asked him why he drew the picture. He said, "I know just how He feels."

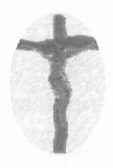

Ronnie's father had a history of being physically abusive; yet Ronnie's self-image still depended on his father's love and acceptance of him. Therefore, in order to secure his father's love, Ronnie had to: (1) repress his hostile impulses towards his father; (2) turn his hostility against himself in the form of self-punishing actions; and (3) believe that his own lack of worth was somehow responsible for his father's violent and erratic behavior. In short, he idealized his father and devalued himself in his doomed quest for fatherly affection.

In the long term, the plan was to help Ronnie get in touch with his repressed anger and avoid the "defense" of turning his hostility against himself. As Freud pointed out, "the origin of depression is in turning against oneself the aggression one cannot direct against its true target, the lost love object."

Ronnie would need considerable emotional support from the staff and a clinical strategy that would help him to see that his perceived worthlessness did not cause his father's hostility and his role as a martyr would not win his father's approval or love. At some point, Ronnie would need to look in other places for love and to approach the search with a heightened maturity.

26. RICHARD: *The Dream*

I had a good relationship with Richard's mother, and the three of us frequently met over the years for conferences about Richard's behavior and progress.

Once in time-out, Richard told me about a dream he had: "I dreamed I was 30 years old and my wife was calling you to tell you what I was doing wrong!"

A major trauma in Richard's childhood was separation from his father at eight years of age. His parents had quarreled and separated. Richard had many difficulties in school, but was conspicuously successful as a negotiator. He was tireless in his efforts to resolve differences between the two sides of any dispute in which he was involved, and usually successful in avoiding an open rupture between the two parties.

Richard's separation from his father had given rise to an intense longing that his parents stop fighting and reunite so that they could all be together again. Throughout his stay at our school, he worked to keep students together so that they wouldn't separate, as his parents had done.

After Richard graduated from our high school, he went on to college, received his Bachelor's degree in Psychology, and eventually graduated from law school with top honors. A childhood trauma resulted in a useful vocational choice in adult life.

27. STEWART : *Now Hear This*

Stewart was a 10-year-old boy, who was in our school for about 4 years. He was well above average in I.Q., but sometimes he would lose control of his emotions and behavior, frequently requiring time-out from the classroom.

During one of many time-outs, Stewart was very agitated and began a verbal diatribe, shouting loudly, in a hostile manner, telling the whole world how angry he was, and why.

When I was able to reflect on this, I wanted to verify his feelings and show support:

Me: "I can see how angry you are."

Stewart: "You mean you can't *hear* how angry I am?!!"

Metaphorically Speaking

Often, in trying to "connect" with the students, I illustrate the situation with metaphors. Sometimes that can be very helpful. For example, with Stewart, if he received a bad grade on a test, it made him feel angry and unacceptable. He would try to insult the teacher and make her feel angry and unacceptable, too.

On one such occasion, I tried to help Stewart see his acting out in perspective, by using an illustrative example.

Me: "Your feelings are like a hot potato that you can't hold onto — you have to 'toss them' to someone else."

Stewart: "Just give it to me straight, Doc — no metaphors, please!"

Little Brown Book

I keep a small, wallet-sized brown note card holder with a supply of 3x5 cards with me at all times. The manufacturer calls it a "mini-briefcase." Every evening, I list all the things I have to get done the following day — parents to call, items that need purchasing or repair, and so forth. Frequently during the day, I add to the list and cross off completed chores. It works for me. Misplacing that little "briefcase" has caused me almost as much anxiety as misplacing my wallet.

On another occasion when Stewart was in time-out, I came to relieve the teacher who took him there.

Me: "Can you tell me what happened, Stewart?"

Stewart: "What for? What good does it do to tell you what happened? All you do is say supportive things and write stuff in your little brown book."

Learn From My Mistakes

I recall leaving my office and thinking on my way to time-out that Stewart's behavior was impossible. I had just made an agreement with him, and now he was back in time-out, one hour later! What did he think he was doing? Didn't I just encourage him by saying that I had confidence in his ability to handle himself without returning to time-out? Why, I thought, was he doing this to me? I was frustrated!

Me: "Why are you back in time-out?"

Stewart: "Why do you write stupid lists in your little brown book?"

Me: "I don't have time for this. Stewart, you need to regroup, as we agreed, so you can return to your class and I can return to my office."

Stewart: "I see you have enough time to get mad at me and forget the purpose of your job."

Me: "Stewart, I'm not mad at you. I just want you to stop making the same mistakes and begin to learn from them."

Stewart: "Well, I just want you to stop getting mad at me so you can learn from my mistakes!"

Stewart was a gifted ten-year-old who was preoccupied with the fear that if he lost control over a situation, others would take advantage of him. He spoke extremely cautiously, in a slow, measured cadence, and resented it when he felt that others interrupted him. Stewart's conversational style controlled the tempo of the encounter, and at times he appeared to be less interested in being understood and more focused on continually having the floor.

A breakthrough seemed to occur when the two of us discussed the themes of our time-out conversations. Stewart disclosed that the tales revealed a basic problem in his life: the mistrust he felt toward others. For the next two years, he tried to guard against his tendency to be mistrustful. By the time he left, after four years at the school, he attributed some of his success to examining how his humor provided a clue as to what was troubling him.

Each one of Stewart's time-out tales contains an unexpected reversal. It is often unavoidable to be both amused and influenced by the funny responses. Metaphors in time-out can be valuable aids in communicating with a student in crisis. Stewart's comments about metaphors were a reminder that it is easy to overuse them, when one is not sure of the ability to use descriptive language to communicate an important point. It is also easy to underestimate a student's ability to understand the issue without an illustration.

Reviewing the encoded messages in the rest of Stewart's tales makes two other lessons apparent. First, at times others may perceive one as being more interested in remembering (taking down notes) than thinking. The need to be seen as a "great rememberer" can be a defense against the embarrassment of being in encounters one cannot control or influence. Second, when Stewart was disrespectful, it was usually because he felt disrespected by an adult. Body language, eye contact and tone of voice can seem disrespectful to a student, even if one is not conscious of feeling that way.

Since I revealed my frustration and anger to Stewart, he felt it was unfair to expect him to conceal his frustration and anger from me. Thus, being angry or uptight leaves one less prepared to assume a helping role than when one is relaxed. It is important to make more of an effort to take a deep breath and relax before entering time-out. This type of presence communicates the message, "It is an opportunity, not a chore, to be in time-out with you."

28. K. C.: *Name-Caller*

K. C. repeatedly called a boy in his class names until he was finally removed from the class and taken to time-out.

Me: "What's wrong, K. C.? Why were you calling Marvin names?"

K.C.: "Why wouldn't I? You should know – *you* don't like him either!"

Me: "What makes you think I don't like him?

K.C.: "Well, you put him in time-out yesterday."

Me: "That doesn't mean I don't like him – and if you think about it, I didn't call him any names either."

K.C.: "Well, that's because you're an a--hole!"

K.C. was incapable of recognizing within himself some of the harsh, attacking feelings that he attributed to others. It was difficult for him to be aware of his hostile side because it was disturbing for him to see the kind of hostility in himself that he resented so much in his father when he got angry and abusive with K.C.

Staff working with K.C. needed to be aware that if he were challenged in time-out, for example, as a consequence for name-calling, he would become even more aggressive. The increased verbal and/or physical aggressiveness was an indication that K.C. perceived a loss of control. At this point, it was important for staff to back off and reassure K.C. that by relaxing and avoiding threatening statements he could re-establish control over the situation as well as himself.

Over time, K.C. was able to experience his relationships with the crisis staff as different from his relationship with his father. K.C.'s progress did not move in a clear linear manner. He continued to use name-calling to establish his dominance when he perceived a loss of control. However, he gradually became more aware of vulnerable aspects of himself that were previously denied rather than acknowledged.

29. MENDEL: *Mistaken Identity*

Mendel, an orthodox Jewish student, was being escorted to time-out for physically aggressive behavior. As he passed by a classroom, he glimpsed Calvin, an African-American student, who had an odd gait, and tended to bob his head as he walked.

Calvin's rhythmic mannerism looked similar to the "*dovening*" (bowing) that is done during the Jewish prayer service.

Mendel: "That's funny – I didn't know Calvin was Jewish!"

Mendel's sarcasm was one way to quiet the fear of his own and his family's history of mental illness. Mendel's older brother was schizophrenic and "rocked" under pressure. In light of seeing the student rock, and being reminded of the disturbing reality of mental illness, Mendel amused himself by pretending to be confused about the other student's religious identity. In pretending that this non-Jewish boy was part of the Yeshiva program where *dovening* was part of the routine, Mendel introduced a funny substitute image for his anxiety-provoking feelings.

Basically, Mendel was telling himself that his own fear of "going crazy" was not a serious concern; in fact, it was really something to laugh about. In this way, Mendel diverted attention from his conflict, and changed the focus from finding fault with himself to finding humor in the imperfections of others. On occasion, Mendel would repeat this tale to me. By repeating it, he provided himself with a safe emotional outlet for his fears and transformed chronic disturbing images into a few seconds of amusement. Laughter reassured Mendel that his fear of going crazy was groundless, and that no one, including himself, could detect his underlying discomfort.

30. SOL: *And the Winner is...*

Sol was an 11-year-old Orthodox Jewish boy in time-out for fighting with Adam, another Orthodox Jewish boy. Sol had accused the other boy of teasing him.

When I got to time-out, Sol had drawn a picture of a man with a long beard and a big hat and another picture of a man with just a *yarmulke* (Jewish skullcap) on his head. The bearded man had his hands raised up in a gesture of "victory."

Me: "Sol, what does your picture represent?"

Sol: "Adam had the nerve to say that his father, who isn't even a *rabbi,* could beat up my father, a *Lubavitcher Rabbi* who follows the teachings of Rabbi Menacham Mendel Schneerson!"

Sol had a diagnosed problem of stuttering in addition to having emotional difficulties. He was overly controlling, self-righteous and confrontational, and was difficult to manage at school. For example, Sol frequently accused the teacher or his peers of some trivial matter. Then he presented his case with intense anger and aggression in an effort to prove that he had a better point than his opponent.

It was revealing that in time-out Sol drew a picture in which his father was the victor — a "stand-in" for Sol himself. Sol's effort to prove that he was right, and others were wrong, was rooted in part in his insecurity regarding his stuttering. Sol wanted others to think that he was in complete control — the "champion" — to compensate for his inability to use words effectively. The illustration provided him with a temporary image of being in control, thereby warding off the fear of being vulnerable to ridicule.

The use of Sol's drawing was a helpful aid in breaking through his resistance to verbalizing the issues that led to his time-out. This was especially so, because Sol was most comfortable when he was not pressured to use words. At the end of our time-out discussion, Sol was able to understand that his father's "boxing victory" represented himself as a "winner." However, the victory was short-lived if he continued to treat others in the same contemptuous manner he feared others would treat him if he stuttered. The illustration allowed Sol to see in his drawing some of the factors that triggered his time-out episodes.

31. ALVIN: *Alternative Medicine*

Alvin, age 15, a new student at the school, was in time-out after he had initiated a fight with another student in gym class.

Me: "Alvin, what happened?"

Alvin: "Dr. Roth, a boy in gym fouled me, and I hurt my knee. Can you take a look at it?"

Me: "I'm not a medical doctor, you know — but since you are walking on it without much difficulty, it is probably not a serious injury. I'll call your mother and see if she can take you to a medical doctor."

Alvin: "What kind of doctor *are* you?"

Me: "I'm a talking doctor."

Alvin: "Well, now I know why they call this an 'alternative' school! But really, I'm worried about my knee. Can't you do *something*?"

Me: "I will get someone to call your mom and get some ice for you to put on your knee. I think you'll be okay for now."

Alvin: "You say I'll be okay, but how would you feel if a 'talking doctor' told you that your knee would be okay?"

Sometimes logical explanations alone are not adequate to help students in crisis. In this tale, the new student's quip reflected his underlying anxiety that he didn't trust me. In some time-out situations, it is not easy to determine how difficult it is for a new student to feel comfortable in one's presence — especially if the interactions with the student have been minimal.

In such cases, it is difficult to recognize one's own contributions to the student's uneasiness. For example, in this tale, Alvin resists telling me directly that he doesn't trust me. Instead, he uses humor to communicate this dynamic indirectly. Clearly, on the surface he is worried about his knee. However, his comment could also be a response to his anxiety about not having a solid therapeutic alliance with me. It can be difficult to sense the atmosphere that is created by these non-verbal dynamics, the way a fish may not feel the water around him; however, it can be self-serving and self-protective to dismiss the importance of these factors.

In this tale, Alvin's facetiousness served both to express and contain his anxiety about his knee and to allow "classified" information ("I can't trust you") to find expression in disguised form.

Comedy is rarely straightforward — it is usually more like the playful definition of a Freudian slip: "You say one thing but you mean your mother." The crisis worker tries to decode the student's verbal antics by listening in a non-defensive manner to both direct and indirect messages.

32. SANTIAGO: *Do-Over*

I was called to remove Santiago from the classroom for threatening other students. While we were walking down the hall, I began asking him some questions.

Me: "What would have been the right thing to do in class, that might have avoided your heading to time-out?"

Santiago: "I'm not sure, but I know what Satan would have done!"

He then started to shove me. At that point, I felt stressed and apparently I must have looked upset. Santiago was taken aback by my demeanor, which was usually more reserved.

Santiago: "Dr. Roth, give me a 'do-over' and I'll do the right thing this time!"

Santiago was referred to our school at the age of eleven because of extremely aggressive behavior. His acting-out consisted of intense yelling and screaming, physically hurting his peers as well as staff, and property damage. At the age of eight years old, Santiago witnessed his mother's death in a car crash. He had been closely attached to her. Santiago's father was emotionally distant and physically abusive, and at age 11, Santiago disclosed this abuse to Social Services. Subsequently, his father lost custody of him, and Santiago was placed in foster care.

Santiago tormented himself for reporting his father to social services. For example, if he heard others talk about their families, it filled him with guilt, regret, and jealousy. At his foster home placement, Santiago was sure that any family to whom he attached himself would abandon him for a "better" child. Accordingly, he could not let any family or any one become important to him.

At school, Santiago's verbal and physical aggression seemed to be a desperate cry for staff to provide immediate comfort and emotional support for his concealed pain. Santiago expected staff to fulfill the role of an idealized mother who would always be there to reassure and console him. His defensive rage could be compared to the screaming of an infant left alone, which serves to call the mother back to the child's side. Santiago expected staff to be always available to him as his mother had been when he was a young child.

This tale caused me to think about what I would do differently in time-out, if I had the chance for a "do-over," in the light of 35 years of teaching and a more realistic view of what is possible. In short, I would devote more time to smiling, relaxing, and trying to appreciate the opportunity to be helpful in crisis situations. Frieda Fromm Reichman said that there were two kinds of patients: those she helped, and those she learned from. Working with students who trigger anger can teach us that each time-out encounter, no matter how stressful, can be a useful learning experience.

33. PETER: *A Test-Taking Strategy*

Peter was a 14-year-old boy who tried to be a very controlling person. On more than one occasion he would manipulate the teacher to send him out of the class in order to avoid taking a test that he did not want to take. On one of these occasions, when I saw him in time-out, I decided to address this issue directly:

Me: "You know, Peter, it's really important to have control over yourself rather than the teacher. Could it be that it's easier for you to start trouble with your teacher than to think about how worried you are about taking a test?"

Peter: "Actually I enjoy every moment of fighting with my teacher! Thinking about a test is not nearly as much fun!"

Manipulation gave Peter the strength to pretend that he was not worried. In time-out, his clever responses kept him from seeing how he did not trust himself any more than he trusted those staff members who failed to succumb to his manipulations. In fact, Peter functioned well below his academic potential at school because his anxiety about failing and his over-controlling manner interfered with his capacity to concentrate and learn.

As the tale reveals, Peter refused to take his manipulative behavior in a serious way. His need to be manipulative blinded him to all other responses that were not similar to his own behavior. It has been said that inside every comedian is a sad man refusing to weep. Peter used humor to exorcise his fear of failure and avoid facing disturbing truths about himself.

Manipulators, like gamblers, do not win each time, but they still enjoy playing the game. Peter liked playing the game; and my presence in time-out conferred recognition and legitimacy to his quest to upset everyone who expected him to reach his potential. Beneath the surface of Peter's manipulative behavior, school represented only one more place where he had to conceal his sense of helplessness and fear of failure. What this helps us to acknowledge is that schools are full of manipulative children who need us to support them and recognize how deep down they struggle with conflicted and self-contemptuous feelings.

34. CY:

Practicing

Cy was a 12-year-old Orthodox Jewish boy. When brought to time-out one day, for spitting on another child's *keepah* (*yarmulke* or skullcap), he began to recite the holy prayer for the dead:

Cy: "*Yisgadal, v'yiskadash, sh'may rabah...*"

Me: "Why are you saying that?"

Cy: "To practice for your funeral if you don't let me out of here!"

For Whose Sake?

As per a clinical intervention suggested by the author Victor Frankel in *Man's Search for Meaning*, I would sometimes ask a student who was struggling to recover his self-control, "For whose sake do you do so?" According to Frankel, if the student responded by saying, "For God's sake," then such a question revealed the depth of the student's personality and religious connectedness. Orthodox Jews, however, refer to God by the name "*Ha-shem*".

Cy was sent to time-out for cursing at his teacher.

Me: "For whose sake should you stop yourself from cursing at the teacher?"

Cy: "Don't tell me I should stop cursing for *Ha-shem's* sake — I don't always agree with Him!"

In crisis situations, Cy used biting sarcasm as if it were a verbal exclamation point. He felt that this transformed him from a position of vulnerability (being sent to time-out) to a position of strength, in which he clearly had the last word. Cy often crossed the line that separated something funny from something destructive. However, just as the stomach of a starving child grows distended, Cy's sarcasm "inflated" when he wasn't fed a diet of reassurance and emotional support.

Cy's reference to *Hashem* revealed his strong connectedness to religion, despite his irreverence (spitting on a *keepah*) and other problematic behavior. In the first tale, Cy attempted to get rid of his conflicted religious feelings by making light of the holy prayer for the dead. The implication was that he was only being funny. Thus, in a situation where he really felt guilty, he could use sarcasm to convince himself that his religious lapses were not serious. In the second tale, Cy's goal was to transform guilt and anxiety about his own lapses in religious observance into sarcastic comments, because in those moments, brief as they were, he could enjoy a feeling of having the "upper hand."

35. RICO: *Intake*

Rico spent many an episode in time-out, but the most amusing incident happened before he even started at our school. Rico was a 14-year-old African American youth when he came to us for the initial interview with his grandmother, who had raised him since he was an infant. He had been unsuccessful in several other schools. He was reluctant about coming to a school with a Jewish name, and he balked at signing the intake papers. I tried to explore his resistance.

Me: "Rico, can you explain why you feel so resistant to coming to our school?"

Rico: "In my [inner-city] neighborhood, I know the kids would make fun of me for going to a 'Jewish' school."

Rico's grandmother wanted very much for him to come to this school, and tried to convince him that his resistance was ill-founded.

Grandmother: "Look at it this way — in many ways, you *are* Jewish."

Rico: "What are you talking about? You know I'm not Jewish."

Grandmother: "Yes, that's right — but you have all the qualities of a Jew: You're smart. You're sophisticated. You're cheap. And you're manipulative."

Rico: "You know, now that I think of it, maybe it wouldn't be so bad if I went to this school." He signed the papers.

Stereotyping is never appropriate, but in this case, the comment served to kick down the door to Rico's resistance. Above the surface, it represented the devotion and concern of a loving grandmother; below the surface, it represented entrenched feelings that would not be funny if they had been directed at an individual or were delivered in a hostile or belittling manner.

In this tale, religious stereotyping was hardly the ideal strategy to defeat Rico's resistance to enrolling at our school; but when all else failed, his grandmother did what she had to do. In part, this approach worked because she believed that her opinion of Jewish people matched that of everyone else's. She was not trying to demean anyone, as she knew that I was Jewish, and her goal was not to insult me. She felt she was simply stating obvious facts. As the matriarch of her family, she rarely encountered people who disagreed with her opinion, so she assumed that Rico, and even I, thought the same way.

Confronting her would have been useless, and each time I tried to think of something diplomatic to say, I was too concerned that I would laugh out loud, so I decided not to say anything.

36. LOUIS: *It's Official*

Louis was a ten-year-old boy in our elementary school, who frequently lost control and became physically aggressive, kicking and yelling in class, and requiring transfer to time-out. Whenever I came into time-out he would always say, "I hate you, Dr. Roth! I don't want you around me! I hate you!" Any attempts to get him to talk were invariably met with, "I hate you! I hate you!"

One time when I came in to help the time-out teacher because Louis was kicking and being particularly aggressive, I countered his extreme aggressiveness with what I thought was an especially calm, soothing approach.

Me: "Louis, there is nothing you can say that will make me angry. I know you always say you hate me, but I'm just going to help you relax and make a good recovery so that you can return to class."

Louis (after he had finally quieted down): "Okay... Now I OFFICIALLY hate you!"

Louis was another youngster who had been removed from his home due to an abusive father. His pattern was to rant against an authority figure, releasing the resentment that he was not able to express to his father. If there were no hostile adult around for Louis to hate, he would have created one for that purpose. Louis expected others to get angry with him, as did his father; however, when staff did not overreact he tried even harder to create a power-struggle, which he then used to justify his belief that all adults were punitive.

Louis' underlying fear was that without identifying others as the enemy, they would be able to examine his personality more critically. They might see how vulnerable he really felt. Accordingly, a comment such as "I hate you" served to keep others at a safe distance. Louis needed to confront and work through his unresolved relationship with his father, so that staff's reaction to his provocations did not remind him of the conflicted relationship he had with his dad.

As an aside, when appropriate to the situation, I try to use humor to help students relax. With Louis, this approach had the opposite effect, making him even more hostile. He feared that laughing would make him look weak, as if he lacked the strength to fight with me. For Louis, not laughing, and saying "I hate you," were defense mechanisms he used in order to ward off defeat.

37. WILLIE: *Say What?*

Willie was a nine-year-old inner-city youngster, living with his single mother, when he was referred to our school. He was openly jealous of his mother's boyfriends, and he showed a pattern of trying to "discredit" his mother. For example, he talked about her drug use, rather than focusing on his own problems.

Once, at a parent conference, the three of us were discussing Willie's problems together. Willie and his mom were arguing about everyone's expectations of him. Willie resorted to his usual defense, trying to "turn the tables" on his mother and focus on her issues instead of his own.

Willie: "You don't care about me! You only care about your boyfriend!

Mother: "That's not true! How can you say that?"

Willie: "Like the other night when you were in the bedroom with your boyfriend and I heard him say, 'Ooooooh Looooorrrrrd! He's coming! He's coming!'"

Willie's mother was taken aback by that, and was very upset and embarrassed. She accused him of making up a ridiculous lie, and profusely denied that any such thing ever happened. She turned to me and said the boy was "watching too much TV, and there's too much sex on TV, and he must have heard that on TV, and made it up," to embarrass her and put her on the defensive.

Willie *insisted* he was telling the truth! I tried to help sort it out.

Me: "Willie, when did this happen?"

Willie: "The other night! I was walking down the hall to Mom's room and her boyfriend heard me walking. That's when he said, 'Ooooooh Looooorrrrrd! He's coming! He's coming!'"

As is the case with many disturbed students, their parents can supply the background information for their children's problems, but they do not supply the exclusive motive or cause. It was important for me to be an impartial voice for both Willie and his mother. There is no way to know the extent to which Willie's behavior was influenced more by personal factors or by factors related to his mother. Typically, Willie fought self-awareness because recognition of his possessiveness and jealousy might upset his idealized self-image. He needed to be "perfect" so that his mother would love him and not leave him for another man.

When Willie started to blame his mother, to divert attention from his own problems, the accusations reinforced his mother's anxiety about her poor mothering skills. That is why she misinterpreted his comment, "He's coming!" The confusion was rooted in her anxiety about being blamed and her fear that the accusations would never stop, no matter what she did, even for things that might have happened in the privacy of her own bedroom.

38. MOSHE: *Inconspicuous*

Moshe was a 16-year-old Orthodox Jewish boy who was significantly emotionally disturbed. He often made bizarre references or made up names for staff members. In time-out, he often called me strange names such as "Professor Munch-kin-stein."

When one of the Orthodox teachers at the school lost a family member, I went to the house to pay my respects. I was somewhat ill at ease, since I am not Orthodox and I am not skilled at all the rituals, such as *dovening* (bowing during prayer). I had planned to stay at the periphery of the ceremony so as not to draw attention to myself.

As I walked in and asked for a *yarmulke* to wear, I noticed that Moshe was also in attendance. As soon as he spotted me, he called out, "Look who's here! Chancellor Stromboli!" Therein ended my opportunity to remain inconspicuous.

It seemed that Moshe selected references or names that represented the qualities he perceived in either the person or the situation. If, for example, I made an effort to talk to him when he did not want to talk, he might call me a mule or a donkey — an animal that was not very smart. Or, he might casually ask me if I had "20/20 vision" if he felt I did not "see" a situation from his point of view. Why Moshe referred to me as "Chancellor Stromboli" or any of the many other names he called me remains a mystery — but it forced me to take a participatory stance in a social situation where I wanted to remain inconspicuous.

My desire to be a spectator, rather than a more active participant, may seem to be inconsistent with my role as principal, where it is necessary to take charge. That said, to be a spectator is as much a stance as to be a participant. As Aristotle said, "The Master and the Slave are tied to different ends of the same chain."

In this light, both the acting-out student and his reticent teacher are tied to different ends of the same bond. Both seek in themselves a strength and courage that might be unattainable without the other. The reckless excess of the student who acts out can stir the outgoing side of the teacher, just as social situations of discipline and ritual can bring out his reserved manner. In short, instead of catching lightning in a bottle, students who act out create the conditions under which others are able to let the lightning out of the bottle.

39. IGOR: *Hide and Seek*

Igor was only 11 years old, an Eastern European immigrant to our country. He had only been in school a few weeks when he began scavenging dictionaries, which he found at other students' desks, and hid them everywhere — under his desk, behind the book cabinet, and many other places.

When I confronted him on the matter, he said, "If I own enough dictionaries, I'll remember all the words and be able to speak good English."

Igor spent several years at the school, and often made clever and amusing observations in time-out and elsewhere. He eventually began participating in the theatrical plays that we put on every spring. Once, in the middle of rehearsing a school play, one of the crew members passed gas. He apologized, saying it was an accident.

Igor: "I don't think you can call it an accident until you're 80."

Igor's general mood could be characterized by recalling Thoreau's famous phrase: "Quiet desperation." Outwardly, Igor needed others to reassure him, and he did so by engaging them in conversation. At school, he felt anxious when his teacher was upset and would start asking her many random questions, without any interest in hearing the answer, so he could be reassured that she was not upset with him. He seemed always fearful of disapproval and responded as though others were trying to belittle him.

Taking dictionaries was Igor's way to communicate his wish that if only he could speak better English, he would have a sense of belonging at the school, and would then obtain the approval he sought. In and of itself, speaking better English could not compensate for Igor's lack of self-confidence. Over time, though, he gained self-confidence because the school made substantive changes in his curriculum; but he also made substantive changes in himself. As evidenced in the second part of this tale, Igor's sophistication and command of English significantly improved. Like most sophisticated humor, it gets at the truth by revealing the information that most of us would prefer to conceal.

40. TODD: *Home Alone*

Todd was a nine year-old boy frequently sent to time-out during his reading period. He was a bright boy, but had a severe reading problem which left him reading at a level much lower than his learning levels in other areas. It seemed that he might be "manufacturing" problems during reading so that he would be sent to time-out and avoid confronting his reading assignment, hence reinforcing his reading problems.

Todd's father had passed away when he was six. He was frequently left in the care of his older sister while his mother was at work.. Their mother would leave notes on the refrigerator with instructions for his sister. When it became apparent that Todd's reading problem might be at the root of his behavior problems, I asked him about it.

Me: "What would happen if you *were* able to read?"

Todd: "Then my mother would be able to leave notes on the refrigerator for *me* — and my sister wouldn't have to stay home and take care of me. I would be left home all alone."

For Todd, the trauma of losing his father not only upset his mental health, but adversely affected his school progress.   Asking the question, "What would happen if...?" resulted in identifying what Todd tried to avoid (abandonment) by not learning to read. Subsequently, Todd's response in time-out turned out to be an initial step toward discussing other factors, unrelated to reading, that inhibited his progress at school.

In time-out, one has a unique opportunity to help students observe forces at work within themselves, when these forces have previously been concealed from their awareness. By asking the question, "What would happen if...?" I learned that Todd had been responding to his fear of abandonment by perpetuating a reading problem that increased his sense of safety. An inability to read was his defense against his fear of being left alone. The defense helped Todd maintain the illusion that his mother and sister would never be able to leave him alone, as long as he remained unable to read. If he were able to read, all hope would be lost for his mother and sister to continue to support and love him in the manner he so desperately needed.

41. KYLE: *Extreme Anxiety*

Kyle was an extremely anxious 14-year-old boy who spent his four years of high school with us. He had such extreme anxiety that it frequently caused him to have bowel problems. Occasionally, when he was so anxious and out of control it was necessary for us to help him clean up and change his pants. He often acted out with defensive anger after these episodes.

Over time, as his bowel accidents decreased, Kyle became convinced that he had more control over himself and the anxiety-provoking situations that led to these accidents. The following exchange took place during a later incident when I was helping Kyle change his pants:

Me: "Kyle, some day you will grow out of this problem — until then we can discuss the best way to handle your anger and shame about returning to class."

Kyle: "Dr. Roth, you can help me change my pants, but you *can't change me!*"

Kyle was a dependent student who solicited help from staff but could not tolerate feeling obligated to them. When he felt obligated, as he did in this tale, he used critical and sarcastic comments to eschew any real engagement with the very person to whom he felt obligated. Interestingly, after making such comments, Kyle would tug at his collar (in much the same manner as did the comedian, Rodney Dangerfield) as if he were trying to shake out his anxiety and look relaxed. In this tale, it became more evident that Kyle's crippling anxiety was, in part, a result of his life-long struggle with the tension between his need to have others help him and his denial of that need.

Kyle never confronted or grieved his father's lack of acceptance of him. He brought to his relationships with males the expectation that they, too, would be emotionally unavailable to him. Kyle's father was Mr. Jackson. Kyle had been taken away from him by the state and placed in a foster home. As a result, Mr. Jackson felt distant from his son. He would only see him for supervised visits a few times each year, such as on birthdays and at Christmas.

Mr. Jackson called me every morning at exactly 7:00 and questioned me about how his son had done the previous day. He would always start out with "Hello. This is Jackson. How's my son doing?" I would give him an update on how things were going with his son, and then he would give me an update on his ongoing court battles with the state agency to try and regain custody of Kyle. These daily conversations would last no more than one minute, and continued throughout the entire four years that his son spent at our school.

Mr. Jackson was given authorization by the state to attend his son's high school graduation. After the ceremony we exchanged small talk. Then he shook my hand and said, "Well, now that Kyle has graduated, does this mean I can't call you anymore?" I was taken aback by this, but I told him he was welcome to call me any time. He did continue to call, a couple of times each month. He would give me an update on how he thought Kyle was doing during their supervised visits, and court battles. He died of a heart attack without ever having Kyle returned to his custody.

42. JAMIE: *No Apparent Trigger*

Jamie was a 10-year-old who was depressed and prone to cry easily. His teacher sent him to my office to talk with me, because he started crying in class. There did not seem to be any apparent trigger for his crying. As a matter of fact, the teacher indicated that he had been doing very well in class that day.

Me: "What's wrong?"

Jamie: "I had a terrible day in class!"

Me: "Tell me more about it."

Jamie: "I can't — it was too terrible."

Me: "Well, something must have been difficult for you in class. It's hard to figure out because your teacher said she came to your desk at least three times and told you that you were doing well."

Jamie: "That's just it! First the teacher comes to my desk three times! Then I'm sent to the principal's office! And you ask me what's so terrible?!"

Jamie had experienced a number of very disturbing events at each of the four schools he had previously attended. By the time he was referred to our school, Jamie presented himself as if he were a victim — constantly hanging his head, and frequently withdrawing into his own private world. For Jamie, it was upsetting when good fortune knocked on his door. Since his identity and self-esteem were closely tied to failure, failure was less frightening to him than experiencing the world in a successful but completely different and unexpected manner.

If Jamie were to embrace his successes at our school, then no one would know the difficulties he had had in all of his previous school placements. Jamie's conflict was not unlike that of a Holocaust survivor who is torn between the desire to put the past behind him, and his pledge never to forget his traumatic past. In Jamie's case, the disturbing stories from his experiences at four other schools were memorialized in symbolic form through his re-creation of failure at his present school, even if circumstances warranted a different and more positive response. Jamie's actions gave special meaning to the adage, "A symptom is a memorial to one's suffering."

43. FRANK: *Bad Luck*

Frank was sent to time-out for a screaming outburst in class, in which he forcefully demanded that the teacher remove all the students from the class who were annoying him.

Me: "Frank, we cannot change the behavior of your classmates, or remove them all. What we *can* do is talk about your feelings so that their annoying behavior will not bother you so much."

Frank: "When Mrs. Taylor resigned last month and I got upset, we talked about it in time-out. When I got angry and cursed at the teacher's aide, we talked about it in time-out. When I got into a fight with Peter after he made fun of me, we talked about it in time-out. But I'm still coming to time-out! Dr. Roth, maybe you're bad luck for me. Can I talk to someone else?"

In this tale, Frank alternated between his feeling of closeness to me and his need for distance. A single time-out encounter can symbolize a student's main conflict. Frank desperately wanted closeness and approval from his peers, and yet when he obtained it, he recoiled because he feared that if he became too close, he would feel trapped, vulnerable, and more easily attacked.

Similarly, as the tale reveals, Frank related to adults in the same manner. He sought their acceptance and support, and yet when he obtained it, he distanced himself from them. This contradiction makes sense by recalling an example cited by the philosopher Arthur Schopenhauer. He observed that on cold winter nights, porcupines huddled together to stay warm. As they drew closer together, they poked each other with their quills, so they recoiled. As they recoiled, they got cold again, and then moved closer once again to stay warm. In this tale, Frank alternated between the pain of being too close and the coldness of being distant.

44. LORENZO: *Can't stop*

Lorenzo was screaming and yelling as I arrived at timeout to help the crisis teacher.

Me: "Lorenzo, we can talk as soon as you stop screaming and yelling."

Lorenzo: "I can't stop! Let me out of time-out and I'll stop!"

Me: "When you are able to stop screaming and yelling, then we can talk."

Lorenzo: "I told you, I can't stop until you let me out of here!"

Me: "But I know you *can* stop. Then we can talk, and then you may come out of the time-out room and go back to class. Okay?"

Lorenzo: "I can't do that!" he replied.

Me: "Why do you think you can't?"

Lorenzo: "Can't you see I'm out of control?!!"

Like an adult who uses drinking as an excuse to act-out without shame, guilt or consequence, Lorenzo perceived time-out as a safe place to use excuses. For example, "Well, I'm in time-out, so what do you expect?" From his point of view, by exposing the foolishness of someone in authority who actually expected him to stop screaming and yelling, he was justifying his actions.

At school, Lorenzo's hypersensitivity left him prone to perceive minor stressors as catastrophic. Moreover, his overreactions to perceived injustices developed a foundation for his volatile relationships with peers and staff. Lorenzo's mother constantly criticized him for failing to meet his school and home responsibilities. The validity of her charges had less impact on him than the hostile manner with which they were spoken. In fact, it became the same hostile and abrasive manner that characterized Lorenzo's interactions with staff and students.

Lorenzo's sensitivity and reactivity confused and frustrated those who tried to help him. It seemed to help when we suggested, "Lorenzo, you may get very upset when frustrating things happen. You can stay upset or you can see that these things happen and are a part of growing up. Try to understand that even if you have some very strong feelings, you can take steps so that these feelings do not get in your way."

45. JACOB: *A Long Stay*

Jacob was an Orthodox Jewish boy who was in our high school for four years. One day, Jacob was being very rude to his teacher—so much so that it was necessary to send him to time-out.

After he calmed down, we discussed and reflected on the misbehavior that got him into time-out. Then he made an observation:

Jacob: "I know I've been in this school too long when I hear myself saying, 'We can agree to disagree!'" (That is one of my more well-worn phrases.)

Jacob was an insecure student, who felt easily threatened. To Jacob there was no security in agreement or compromise; there was only security in opposition and defiance. Jacob needed to defeat authority figures so he could be relieved of his inner doubts and feelings of insecurity. Jacob's rebelliousness was directed mainly toward staff that he perceived did not like him. This brings to mind the maxim that in order for a student to develop a therapeutic relationship, he does not need to like you but he does need to feel either that you like him or, at least, that you do not *dis*like him.

By opposing authority, Jacob found security in a feeling of being right and of being superior, without having to acknowledge those aspects of himself which were threatening — that is, his self-doubt and deep insecurity. Nietzsche said,

> "Perhaps I know best why it is man alone who laughs.
> He alone suffers so deeply that he had to invent
> laughter. A joke is an epitaph to a disturbing emotion."

In time-out, Jacob's comment to me was an epitaph to his disturbing emotion, that is, his fear that agreement or compromise might cause him to lose his rebellious identity. Getting me to laugh helped to silence his inner doubt, and gave him a sense of relief that at least for now, his disturbing emotions would not be exposed, and that I still liked him despite his oppositional manner.

46. AARON: *How Would You Know?*

Aaron was an 8-year-old boy in our Orthodox Jewish elementary class. He was not violent or assaultive, but he had a tendency to try and get around rules and regulations.

A parent called up one day and said she would like to get some information:

Parent: "Can you tell me more about the Collection for the Religious School Fund?"

Me: "What fund?"

Parent: "A student of yours, Aaron, has been going around the neighborhood with a collection canister, asking for money for the 'Religious School Fund.'"

I confronted Aaron about the matter.

Me: "Aaron, do you know that it is a crime to collect money as you have been doing?"

Aaron: "What do you know about it? You are just a 'Reform' Jew! You are not Orthodox! You have no knowledge of Jewish law! If you had any knowledge of Jewish law, you would understand! What I'm doing is a *mitzvah* (good deed)."

Me: "How can it be a *mitzvah*? You are collecting the money under false pretenses and you are keeping it for yourself!"

Aaron: "Oh, Dr. Roth! You don't wear even a *yarmulke!* (skull cap). How would you know the difference between a crime and a *mitzvah*?"

Portraying me as an inept Jew was an escape from an emotional burden imposed by Aaron's father, who constantly criticized him for failing to meet his religious obligations. Thus, when Aaron chided me for being non-observant and uninformed, this was actually an effort to divert criticism from himself for not meeting his father's religious expectations. Asking me, "How would you know the difference between a crime and a *mitzvah*?" was Aaron's warning signal to himself of his own lapses from religious observance.

Instead of reading the signals of deeper and more complex issues within himself, Aaron relocated the problem to me, and ridiculed my lack of orthodoxy. Externalizing conflicted feelings can be compared to coal miners' use of canaries to detect dangerous levels of methane gas. The canaries, having weaker respiratory systems, would quickly succumb to the gas. Thus, the miners were warned and had time to exit from the danger. If the miners had acted as though the solution were to fix the canary, rather deal with the source of the toxic methane, it would have been similar to Aaron's focusing on my shortcomings rather than dealing with his own inner chaos. It has been said that a joke is like a whisper before the shouting starts. Aaron's tale is a whisper before he starts facing disturbing truths about himself in a more straightforward manner.

47. MICHELLE: *Cranky*

Michelle was a 15-year-old girl at our school. One day she was sleeping in class, and when the teacher awakened her, Michelle cursed at her and pushed her away. For that reason, the teacher sent her to time-out.

I met with Michelle in time-out.

Me: "Do you think you acted out in class because you were tired and cranky?"

Michelle: "No! I was only cranky because that little teacher woke me up!"

Michelle presented herself in a detached, impersonal manner.   Her conviction that she would fail was so deep-seated that she often viewed "giving up" as the only way to prevent her situation from getting worse. Michelle felt that the only relief from her discouragement was to hide behind a mask of incompetence so others would make no demands on her.

In this time-out encounter, by being sent out of class for sleeping, Michelle experienced another embarrassing failure. In her reply to me, Michelle excused herself from any responsibility for her actions. Moreover, in class, she used anger as a defense to divert others from detecting her underlying feelings of failure, and of being "less acceptable" than her peers. Anger became her strategy for safeguarding herself from anticipated failure.

Interestingly, most of Michelle's humor contained a reference to "smallness," for example, when she referred to "that little teacher." Although her teacher was of average height, Michelle attributed "smallness" to her and others in an attempt to rise above her feelings of unworthiness. In counseling, it was hard to break through Michelle's mistaken belief that she was worthless. Over time, she would need to acknowledge and take responsibility for her actions in order to gain the courage to change her misguided perception of herself.

48. DUSTIN:

Miranda Rights

Dustin was in time-out for cursing at his teacher.

Me: "Was it necessary to use curse words to express yourself?"

Dustin: "I was just venting!"

Me: "Venting is appropriate in time-out, not in class.

Dustin: "If it is okay to vent in time-out, then anything I say in time-out should not be held against me!"

Late

I was attending to another crisis when I got the call to come and see Dustin in time-out. I went to him as soon as I could stabilize the earlier situation. When I finally got to Dustin, he refused to talk to me.

Me: "I'm sorry it took me so long to get to you, but don't let your feelings about my being late get in the way of our talking with each other."

Dustin: "Well, Doc, my feelings weren't getting in the way until I had to wait so long for you to get here!"

A Touching Story

The school bus driver asked me to speak with Dustin, who he said had been masturbating on the bus. When initially interviewed, Dustin denied the bus driver's accusation. Deciding to take a different tack, I began the following exchange:

Me: "You say you were not touching yourself. But did you have your hands in your pants?"

Dustin: "Well, yes — but only for one minute, and only one hand!"

Dustin, 13 years old, verbally attacked his teachers to gain approval and acceptance from his peers, who otherwise may have rejected him because of his superior academic strengths. A flurry of hostile comments toward a teacher was one way for Dustin to lower himself to what he thought was the level of the class. This strategy forced the students to side with either the teacher or Dustin. In most cases, they sided with the teacher, because of her authority, and because it provided them with an opportunity to put Dustin in his place. When the students sided with the teacher, Dustin's first impulse was to hide his feelings of disapproval behind additional amusing, but hostile, comments, thus renewing the cycle of his inappropriate behavior.

Given that emotional disclosure is not always accomplished directly, students like Dustin communicate their thoughts and feelings more naturally by making jokes. To Dustin, discussing his feelings in a direct manner meant "loss of face." During time-out, comedy was Dustin's way to reverse his feelings of vulnerability, if only for a moment. He transformed vulnerable experiences into amusing ones, in order to extract pleasure from them. The shelf-life of a joke is limited, but its ability to provide momentary gratification without shame or guilt is powerful.

In the tale where Dustin declared his "Miranda rights," he was attempting to find a permissible way of admitting that his language was inappropriate, without being held accountable. In the second tale, wherein I was late to time-out, Dustin uses a humorous comment to divert me from concentrating on his inappropriate behavior, and to divert himself from acknowledging his ambivalence regarding his place at school. Finally, in response to the bus driver's allegations, Dustin used mockery to get rid of the humiliation and embarrassment of getting caught "red-handed."

The meaning behind Dustin's humor may be speculative, and based on a subjective interpretation of complex factors. However, it seems clear that he used it to seek relief by making fun of others and the circumstances of the situation.

49. ALEX: *Revenge*

Alex is a 14-year-old boy who was frequently sent to time-out for his outbursts, and inability to maintain self-control. One time when I went to see him in time-out, he was quite calm, and had already regrouped, and had even started working on an assignment.

Me: "Alex, what happened that caused you to be sent to time-out?"

Alex: "Nothing! I just heard my teacher complaining about all the paperwork she has to fill out when she sends someone to time-out. I just wanted to keep her busy after class."

Alex had heard his teacher complaining about all the extra paperwork and documentation involved whenever a student went to time-out. He chose to exercise his power and cause his teacher's consternation by acting out, going to time-out, and thereby causing *her* to have to stay after class!

Alex and his teacher acted more alike than either realized. The controlling tendencies that they shared contributed to the frustration that each felt toward the other. If they could have acknowledged how their shared tendencies accounted in part for each other's behavior, they would have had a better chance to minimize their ongoing power struggles. Unfortunately, instead of seeing each other's behavior as a mirror, they saw it as a target, and winning battles became the all-important focus.

"To a man with a hammer," said Mark Twain, "everything looks like a nail." To this teacher, almost any behavior Alex presented looked like a time-out; to Alex, almost any directive by the teacher demonstrated her foolishness. Given their problematic relationship, it was important to work with both of them on moving from idealistic to realistic goals, thereby increasing their opportunities for success in their respective roles.

50. FORD: *Whistler's Student*

Ford was six years old when he came to the school. I soon discovered that when he was agitated in time-out, any attempt to confront the problem directly only seemed to escalate him.

Although I have no special ability to sing or play an instrument, I have always been able to whistle a tune fairly well. Some children find this amusing and it can be a very helpful diversionary tactic that keeps their distress at bay.

Ford was amused and enchanted by my whistling, so I always started out in time-out with him by asking him to guess what tune I whistled. It might be the theme from "Looney Tunes" or "Mary Had a Little Lamb" or popular theme songs from TV shows or movies. This was a successful maneuver on a number of time-out occasions, as it would settle him down and allow him to regroup and talk calmly about why he was in time-out.

One day, in time-out, Ford's anger was extremely intense.

Me: "Can tell me the name of this tune?" (I started whistling.)

Ford: "WHISTLING WILL NOT WORK TODAY!! DON'T EVEN TRY IT!!"

With Ford, I was working under a strategy similar to the comedian, W. C. Fields, that is, "If you can't dazzle them with brilliance, baffle them with bull!" Since my "brilliance" did not seem to work, I tried "amusing" Ford with "virtuosity."

Ford's comment to me, "Whistling will not work today!! Don't even try it!!" initially triggered a sense of guilt that I had been wasting his time using a diversionary intervention rather than focusing on the problem itself. Even though reasonable people may disagree on this issue, I wonder whether I may have invested a student with too much power to validate whether I am effective in my role.

In this tale, rather than accepting my offer of entertainment, Ford showed that he was actually starting to develop the courage to face his problems. In fact, when all is said and done, a student's gradual and evolving independence, rather than dependence on the staff, is the most compelling validation that the school and the staff are doing an effective job.

51. LATRELL: *Throw the Book at her*

Latrell was sent to time-out for throwing his book at the teacher's desk and hitting her with it. He felt that the book was "too easy," even though it was appropriate for his reading level. He wanted another book, a more difficult one that another student, Danny, used. In time-out, Latrell and I had the following conversation:

Latrell: "If I'm not given a harder book to read, like Danny has, I'll never do my work again! I'll throw all the 'baby books' at the teacher's face!"

Me: "And if you get the book that you want, and it turns out to be too hard for you, then what will happen?"

Latrell: "Well, if it's too hard, I'll probably throw that at her, too!"

Latrell had no tolerance for ambiguity. He saw school staff as either bad or good, and saw his own problems as not really his fault, but rather the fault of the "bad" staff. Latrell idealized the "good" staff, hoping that they would protect him from those who had evil intentions. When Latrell realized that even the "good" staff would not always do his bidding, his idealized image of them was shattered and then replaced with an image of uncaring, negative adults. It was helpful for staff to be emotionally supportive, rather than focusing on his sarcasm or negativity; and it was useful to coordinate a crisis plan for Latrell among all the staff. That was more likely to prevent him from pitting one staff member against another, by demonizing certain staff and lionizing others in order to exact a saving response from staff he perceived to be on his side.

What Latrell feared most was facing his painful feelings of not being competent enough to do his schoolwork. His humorous comment was an attempt to rescue a conscious feeling of control from an unconscious feeling of inadequacy. I had the opportunity to experience this transformation first-hand. Just as an appreciative audience helps to boost a comedian's self-confidence, Latrell's self-confidence would be boosted by appreciating how hard it was for him to face the feelings of inadequacy that triggered this time-out episode.

52. BERT: *Old News*

Bert was a withdrawn third-grader who had been sent to my office for being abrupt and uncharacteristically sarcastic toward the teacher. The teacher had said he wasn't his usual self today, and maybe he had something he needed to talk about.

Me: "Did something happen before today that bothered you?"

Bert: "Does something always have to happen before something else?"

Me: "Sometimes when you look at things that happened in the past, it makes it a little easier to figure out what has gone wrong in the present."
     Bert thought for a minute, and then noticed the antique-style radio on the cabinet in my office.

Bert: "Is that why you have an antique radio?" he asked, "So you can hear old news and figure out what's happening today?"

Bert's mother had abandoned him when he was five years old. Now Bert was a ward of the state and he presented himself at the school as being shy and withdrawn. Bert became angry and resentful whenever he felt left out at school. In this tale, Bert felt left out because that morning his teacher told him that he had not been selected to represent his class in a school-wide writing contest. In reaction, Bert verbally attacked the teacher. He felt entitled to attack her because he felt that the approval he sought for his writing was not an unreasonable expectation.

Bert was looking for his teacher to be the "good mother" he never had. He held onto the notion that the problems he had with his teacher were rooted in her rejection of him. He was unable to recognize the part he played in his problematic encounters with her. Bert needed to confront the reality that his teacher (and females in general) could not be his idealized mother. In this tale, Bert's question about why I listen to an antique radio was really a concealed blueprint for his therapeutic success. That is, if Bert were to achieve mastery of his grief, he would need to confront the pain of hearing "old news" about himself, and about his mother's limitations.

As long as Bert clung to the notion that females should make up the difference to him, he was destined to misunderstand "what's happening today" in light of his unresolved past. For Bert, the clinical goal at school was to help him find out what to do with all the tension, hostility and sadness that built up inside of him whenever he felt left out or rejected. Otherwise, he would continue to experience his teacher (and all females) as uncaring and rejecting, not recognizing how his resistance to facing "old news" created the very rejection he feared. Eventually, Bert graduated from high school and attended a local university. In therapy, he struggled with letting go of his unrealistic expectations and worked on replacing them with the capacity to become his own good parent.

53. ISHAM: *Mr. Jernigan's Exit*

Isham was upset because his teacher, Mr. Jernigan, just announced that he was leaving the school. Isham had an outburst of temper at hearing this news, and was sent to time-out.

Me: "What upset you about Mr. Jernigan's announcement? I didn't know you would miss him."

Isham: "I won't. I hate Mr. Jernigan. I'm just angry because now our whole class will have to get used to a new teacher."

Me: "Well, that won't be easy — but at least you seem to have some understanding of how the whole class will have to pull together in order to get through this difficult time."

Isham: "Well, right now I don't think the class is all that bad."

Me: "Good! That is a sign of real progress, Isham! In the last two years, I cannot recall your saying anything positive about your class. That is a very good sign!"

Isham: "Not really, Dr. Roth — The only good thing about it is that Mr. Jernigan is going to leave."

My elaborate optimism appeared comical to Isham. He proceeded to provide me with a reality check about what was *really* happening in his class — things were not going well, but he was enjoying it at the moment because of Mr. Jernigan's departure.

At school, Isham's aggressive behavior and language concealed a history of physical abuse. He tended to demonize others without making any effort to understand them. In particular, he lacked patience with adults, and had difficulty understanding their point of view. Isham blamed himself for bringing on the abuse, and on occasions when he had a chance to see his classmates interact happily with their families, it filled him with regret, jealousy and anger. What Isham needed most was a teacher who could be stable and calm in the midst of his aggressive outbursts.

Mr. Jernigan was a veteran teacher who had taught Isham's class for two years. He related to the students in a rigid, inflexible manner. His uncompromising, rule-bound approach created a situation in which the students inevitably resisted him. Then he used their resistance to justify his overly controlling manner. He tried to maintain his self-image as a "concerned-but-tough" teacher, but in the process, he established a pattern in which both he and the students continued to act out their self-defeating roles.

Mr. Jernigan tended to see students as either "all good" or "all bad," and did not conceptualize that a student could have both positive and negative characteristics. He avoided his own disturbing feelings, projected negativity onto others, and tested my ability to manage my own negative reactions toward *him*. In the end, I, like Isham, found myself looking forward to the time when Mr. Jernigan would be gone!

54. GEORGE: *No Way To Please*

George was sent to time-out twice in one day, for verbal conflicts with his teacher. I went to see him both times.

Me: "The first time you were in time-out today, you told me you were angry at Ms. Wilson for talking to you about your work. This time you got angry at her for not paying enough attention to you. It sounds like there is no way for her to please you, and that you will get upset with her no matter what she does. Is that the way you want to deal with Ms. Wilson?

George: "You think you know more about how to handle Ms. Wilson than I do?"

It was difficult to reason with George, because he saw himself as a "school outlaw" — someone who broke all the rules in order to highlight what he saw as foolish policy and uncaring staff. George saw his role as a badge of honor, and expected others to praise and respect him for it.

In family therapy, we tried to encourage George's father to reinforce good behavior with praise when George did well at school. Unfortunately, his father was indifferent to George's social problems at school. It seemed as though his father tried to compensate for his own personal and professional failings by reinforcing George's renegade image. To avoid disappointing him, George rarely allowed himself to develop positive relationships with his teachers. He could not allow a positive relationship to disturb his carefully orchestrated image. George's chronic anger at his teacher represented a tug-of-war between needing to please his father and acknowledging his inherent desire to do well at school.

George's reply to me, "You think you know more about how to handle Ms. Wilson than I do?" can be viewed as an indirect confirmation that he could not accept my comments to him. He felt they were unrealistic, as if I could moderate his intense anger by overpowering him with logical and sequential details. In addition, George was telling me that I could not possibly understand the sense of obligation he felt toward his father, nor his deeply buried fear that he would not be able to escape his identity as a "school outlaw." In short, George's reply to me indirectly communicated his untold story of conflicted feelings and emotional obligation.

George was saying, in effect, "You think you can logically show me the error of my ways, but you don't have a clue about the real details that guide my actions."

55. ALLEN: *Keep It Simple*

Allen was a very insecure 12-year-old. In time-out, I tried to be especially delicate with any criticism. My typical statement to him was, "I like you, but I don't like how you are acting." During one encounter in time-out, we had the following exchange:

Allen: "Dr. Roth, this time I've been so bad, I know you'll stop liking me, right?"

Me: "Allen, I feel that you are concerned that what you did makes you a bad person, and you want me to tell you that I'm still on your side."

Allen: "Is it too much to ask for a simple 'yes' or 'no'?"

Allen loved his father even though he was abusive to Allen's mother, and he was not able to take care of his family. His father frequently left the house for weeks at a time without warning. His father wanted to be able to develop a positive relationship with Allen, in part because he felt so guilty. However, when Allen requested "special time" with him, he never followed through. Allen assumed that his father's lack of follow-through was motivated by his disapproval of him. At school, Allen presented himself as self-critical, lacking self-confidence, and unable to form close, meaningful relationships.

The manner and tone in which Allen responded to me ("Is it too much to ask for a simple yes or no?") had a ring of truth to it, and stirred up sad feelings in me. I tried to let my sadness become a point of departure for identifying possible sad feelings in Allen that were too difficult for him to acknowledge. For example, Allen was sad because his father had not been available to support and nurture him. Likewise, Allen thought I was depriving him of the emotional support he wanted — the same feeling he had in relation to his father.

In this tale, unable to feel the sadness related to his father, because it hurt too much, Allen exerted pressure on me through his sarcasm to experience his unwanted sadness. In reaching within myself, I was better able to understand what Allen was trying to tell me: Was it too much to ask his principal to support and nurture him in an unconditional manner? This tale demonstrates the value of using one's emotional reactions as an important clue about what is going on inside of the student. Such clues can then be used to form a diagnostic impression of the subjective meaning of the student's humorous comments.

56. KRAMER: *Finding Fault*

Kramer: "I hate my teacher and I'll never make it in this school!"

Me: "You have a great future in this school. You just need to free yourself of the need to see your teacher as bad, and stop being disrespectful to her."

Kramer: "I'm not disrespectful! She's an idiot!"

Me: "It's important to remember that you find fault with a lot of people — your teachers, your friends, your family."

Kramer: "Then you're an idiot too, because you want me to give up what I really think!"

At school, Kramer operated under the assumption that if he became too close to others, he would become more vulnerable to rejection. As a result, Kramer's *modus operandi* was to find fault and attack others before they could find fault with him. This strategy denied others the power to hurt or reject him. It was as if Kramer used the art of wisecracking to communicate indirectly his own feelings of vulnerability, undo his disappointment in himself, and regain his shaken self-confidence.

Kramer's final reply to me indicated that he was not about to suffer through one of my interpretations without some type of revenge. His first impulse was to return my perceived criticism of him by one-upping me with a better version of the same disrespect that got him into time-out in the first place. My interpretation, even if accurate, was too threatening for Kramer to process. As a result, he attacked me for attacking him.

This tale served as a useful reminder to me of how an interpretation can be easily misunderstood or perceived as invasive by the very person that we are trying to help. Kramer felt threatened by my comments, and his reply indicated that he wanted to correct me because he thought that I didn't understand him. His hostile reaction to the interpretation was a confirmation that either it was off-target or the timing of it was misguided.

57. JACKSON: *A Good Reason*

Jackson was in time-out for threatening to beat up Vern and refusing to relent when asked to stop. Earlier in class, Jackson had positioned himself so that Vern would get the full impact of his expelling flatus. Vern responded by holding his nose and calling Jackson an emotionally-charged name, and that is when Jackson started threatening to beat him up, eventually having to be sent to time-out.

Me: "Jackson, can you think of anything you might have done that would cause Vern to call you that name?"

Jackson: "Dr. Roth, I don't care what you say, he had no right to call me a mother-f---er, just because I farted in his face. He has to have a *GOOD* reason!"

Jackson, age 12, spent two years at our school. He was referred at age 10 when he had been abandoned by his mother and left at a homeless shelter. At school, when Jackson perceived that he was being treated unfairly, his first response was to get intensely angry and aggressively defend himself. He was so sure that he was not loved or appreciated, that the intensity of his anger had the effect of triggering the very rejection he feared. Instead of confronting the reality of his disturbed feelings, Jackson used defensive anger to bury his internalized conflicts and to conceal his low self-esteem.

In part, Jackson relied on his anger so he could hold onto the hope that someday he would be able to force others to be more appreciative or loving of him. Through angry overreactions, Jackson managed to reassure himself that he was in control, and that he could not be pushed around. In so doing, he recreated with others the same dynamic that characterized his relationship with his family, that is, the sense of being rejected or treated unfairly.

58. CARTER: *Nice Vs. Rich*

In time-out, Carter reflected on the number of times that he had been psychiatrically hospitalized for behavior problems. His father, who was very wealthy, but also very cold and distant, would frequently have him hospitalized when he acted out aggressively.

Carter: "Have you ever been hospitalized, Dr. Roth?"

Me: "No, Carter, I haven't."

Carter: "Are you rich?"

Me: "No."

Carter: "Are you nice to your children?"

Me: "Are you wondering whether I am more like you, hospitalized, or more like your father, rich?"

Carter: "I guess you're not like either one of us. Neither one of us would have come up with an answer like that."

It is a fair question whether a tale like this has any real predictive value as to how a student progresses at school. Carter was trying to evaluate my personality, and beyond that, the personality of the school. The more reassurance and emotional support we could provide, the more resolve Carter would have to view the school as a positive place in which he could grow. The less reassurance and emotional support he received, the more he would be likely to view the school as a negative place in which he would develop an attitude of "What's the use of trying?"

There are certain moments that pull everything together for a student at a specialized school. Carter would sometimes remind me of this tale to highlight his progress. But those are only moments, and far more important than what is *said*, is showing reassurance and emotional support through one's *actions*.

59. STEPHEN: *Accomplish Vs. Overcome*

Stephen came to my office and asked to speak with me.

Stephen: "After four years here, I want to talk to you about something you said to me in time-out that I have always remembered."

Me: "What's that?"

Stephen: "You told me, 'It's not always what you accomplish; It's what you overcome.'"

Me: "What are your thoughts about that?"

Stephen: "That with all your experience, you should know that it's BOTH!"

Stephen was shy, withdrawn, and lacking in self-confidence. His uneasiness and discomfort with himself were reinforced by his father, who communicated intense disapproval of Stephen's passivity. On the surface, Stephen felt obligated to please his father in order to save him any distress or disappointment. Beneath the surface, his anger toward his father for not supporting him was so intense that it required Stephen to make a Herculean emotional effort to conceal it. Encapsulating his anger significantly interfered with Stephen's capacity to experience a full range of emotions.

At school, Stephen felt particularly helpless under the influence of authority figures, and he was preoccupied with what other students thought of him. Basically, he was re-experiencing at school the same feelings of powerlessness that he felt with his father. At times, Stephen tried to engage with his classmates and yet, when this happened, he avoided asserting himself. In therapy Stephen related his fear that if he were more assertive, he might let go of all of his inhibited emotions, especially his anger. Occasionally, this personal Catch-22 led Stephen to withdraw into his own fantasy world. Unfortunately, the fantasy world was more frightening than he could tolerate; and then he exhibited psychotic symptoms.

In the two years that Stephen attended our high school, he accomplished and overcame many obstacles. At the end of his senior year, he had an argument with his father over whether he should pursue a career as a car mechanic, which is what his father wanted, or attend the Big Ten university to which he had been accepted. During the argument, Stephen found the courage to tell his father that he was tired of being under his thumb. This episode became an important turning point for him. As a result, shortly after that incident, Stephen came to my office to remind me, "It's not what you accomplish *or* what you overcome — it's *both*."

In this astute correction, Stephen flexed his assertive muscles and proved to himself that he could overcome his deep-seated pattern of inhibiting his aggressive impulses, especially with authority figures. It is always rewarding when students come to your office and remind you of something you discussed with them during time-out. Haim Ginott said, "Discipline is a series of small victories." Similarly, one can take comfort in knowing that a brief time-out encounter can provide valuable lessons that can be internalized by students in ways that could not have been predicted or imagined.

60. WALTER: *Three Wishes*

Walter, a 12-year-old boy, was sent to time-out for throwing a tantrum in class. He was jealous that another student brought his iPod to school.

Me: "It sounds like you were frustrated that you didn't have an iPod."

Walter: "Sure, why shouldn't I be? I want to be happy too! All I'm asking for is a good school, a nice teacher and a stinkin' iPod."

In discussing how humor can be used to triumph briefly over one's distress, one can easily distance oneself from a student's emotional pain. In this tale, Walter's expectations not only seemed absurd, but probably reflected society's unrealistic and/or materialistic values. Nevertheless, for Walter, as a ward of the state, each day brought more resentment and despair. Unable to grasp what happened to his life, Walter externalized his demoralization in the form of aggressive and intimidating behavior.

Three simple wishes provided Walter with the hope that some day he would be able to live in a sane and ordered world, which to this point was chaotic and beyond his logical comprehension. Over a period of years, Walter was able to use the school to help him develop more realistic and attainable priorities.

61. SID: *Majority Rules*

Sid was sent to time-out because the students in his class voted to do something he did not want to do. Sid reacted by crying, screaming, and belittling himself. He was too upset to stay in class, so his teacher sent him to time-out.

Me: "What happened?"

Sid: "I hate myself! I'm a stupid S.O.B. for being at such a dumb school!"

Me: "While it may appear to you right now that you don't like yourself, to me, you are an intelligent person who got upset in class. Let's talk about why each of us sees you differently."

Sid: "But more people agree with me than they do with you! Everybody thinks that I am a stupid S.O.B. So, the majority rules."

Sid, age 11, had a habit of defending himself by turning the blame upon himself. He was raised by an alcoholic mother and father, and the atmosphere at home was chaotic and unpredictable. Sid was confused about his ability to find trust and security in relationships. When he encountered a setback at school, his first impulse was to belittle himself. He did this reflexively, unaware that he was internalizing anger that was really directed at someone else. At times, his peers were put off by his self-deprecating comments, and they reacted by ridiculing him. Then, Sid would use their attacking responses to confirm his own negative perception of himself.

There are times when being able to say something funny about an upsetting experience can prevent further escalation of the problem. Sid's comment, "So, the majority rules," was a response to an emotionally charged trigger in class that he perceived as upsetting.

Sid's piquant humor disparaging himself disguised his anger at the class. In this tale, the transformative power of Sid's wit was successful because his resistance to a more frank analysis of his true anger was softened. Like all good comedy, Sid's comment helped him to regroup. A momentary stepping back from the real issue can, in the long run, lead to greater emotional stability. After that, Sid was able to talk about the emotionally charged trigger without getting caught up in it. His irony helped to make him less afraid and less guilty in the face of his own hostility toward his classmates.

62. FLETCHER: *The Critic*

During the annual holiday party Fletcher was sent to time-out for rowdy behavior in the auditorium.

Me: "What happened at the party?"

Fletcher: "I was disappointed in the entertainer. The show was better last year!"

Me: "I thought that the entertainer was very good. In fact, some people told me he was better than the person from last year."

Fletcher: "Maybe he was — but I was in time-out, so I couldn't tell you!"

Some students fear time-out because it reinforces their loneliness. To these students, the fear of being alone grows more acute when they are unable to communicate their thoughts and feelings. As a result, during time-out some students use wordplay less as a diversion and more as a pragmatic form of therapy. In this manner, they are able to reconnect with others and offset their fear of finding themselves alone. The attraction of comedy is that it is entertaining and reasonably non-threatening to the teller and to the listener.

In this tale, Fletcher's sarcasm did not substitute for a therapeutic discussion of the rowdy behavior which triggered the time-out. In fact, some may argue that it served no therapeutic value and contributed little, if anything, to his overall understanding of what happened. However, its value was in its ability to take the middle ground — releasing some of the pressure he felt about being ostracized, and at the same time allowing him a momentary release from a one-down position by mocking his own frustrated wishes.

63. DAN: *Wrong, again!*

Me: "Dan, I'm surprised you are in time-out! I just saw your teacher this morning."

Dan: "Really, what did she say?"

Me: "Actually, she gave me a good report about you! That's why I'm surprised to see you here."

Dan: "Well, Dr. Roth, this isn't the first time you've been wrong. That obviously wasn't *my* teacher!"

Dan, age 14, was an unusually thoughtful student who tended to act out when he had an ulterior motive. When I asked Dan if he had noticed that his amusing reply turned the unexpected (receiving a good report from his teacher) into the expected (he would never receive a good report), he thought about it for a moment. Then he related that the good report from his teacher reminded him that he wanted to move forward and return to public school. On the other hand, pretending that this was a case of mistaken identity was his way to convince himself as well as me that he was not ready to be mainstreamed into public school.

Historian D. Boorstein commented, "Trying to plan for the future without knowing the past is like trying to plant cut flowers." In mainstreaming Dan, it would be crucial to take into account his self-doubt, fear and anxiety about returning to public school. Dan's comment, "She obviously isn't my teacher," was an early warning sign that our school should mainstream Dan in a cautious, thoughtful and sequential manner.

64. CARL: *Worst Enemy*

In time-out, Carl told me that he considered his worst enemy to be the student with whom he had just fought in class, which led to his being in time-out.

Me: "Carl, your worst enemy is not your classmate Jake, but your inability to control your anger."

Carl: "As long as YOU are the principal of this school, anger is NOT my worst enemy."

In this tale, Carl diverted attention from his own personal issues and tried to gain momentary gratification by putting me down. Carl was saying that his inability to control himself was not the real problem — I was the real problem. By projecting his vulnerability onto me, Carl tried to get rid of his shame and guilt for initiating the classroom fight.

There is something distressing about the way Carl's comment to me kept him from acknowledging his own personal issues. Many time-out encounters are similar to Carl's — they remain unresolved, incomplete, and in the end, the student does not acknowledge his own complicity. Carl unfortunately fell into that category.

When Carl was 17, he died of a gunshot wound he sustained in a neighborhood gang brawl. Each student who leaves the school without acknowledging, facing and working through his personal issues, reminds me of Carl and his tragic fate. The *Talmud* (a collection of early Jewish writings) says, "To a survivor, one person dies a thousand times." I have probably thought about Carl a thousand times; and wondered what I could have done differently that might have had a positive impact on his fate.

65. DAVID: *Cellularus Interruptus*

I always try to answer my cellphone in time-out as the staff may be calling me for an emergency. I was in the middle of a discussion with David, when my cellphone rang, and I answered it.

David: "Excuse me, Dr. Roth! Was I boring you?"

David perceived my interruption as an insult, since I didn't excuse myself before answering the phone. David was making it easier for me to understand his hurt feelings by transforming them into a sarcastic comment. In this manner, he was trying to preserve our positive relationship, which he had come to value. Why didn't he just blurt out that I made him angry because I didn't put him first? The joke was a way for him to tell me that without my getting angry and jeopardizing our relationship.

It is important to remind oneself that every individual in the school — staff and student — has feelings that can be easily hurt. Sometimes, when we are expected to juggle several responsibilities at the same time, there is the risk of saying or doing something that is abrupt or rude. As professionals, we have to be sensitive to these unintended actions, and equally sensitive to the manner in which humor can be used to alert us to our insensitivity. Unsuspecting staff who do not attribute symbolic significance to whimsical comments may be providing themselves with an excuse to avoid looking at their own blind spots, and how their personal actions or words may have, in part, provoked the student in an unintended manner.

In this manner, understanding a student's wit sometimes forces difficult introspection, but it also provides a variety of opportunities for personal growth and development. This tale from time-out was such an opportunity. It provided a chance to rediscover how admitting my insensitivity ("David, I'm sorry I didn't excuse myself before I took the phone call. How did that make you feel?") could provide significant value in exploring with the student how our interaction is mutually influencing.

66. RICKY: *Delayed Transmission*

Ricky was in time-out for cursing at his teacher.

Me: "What did you really want to tell the teacher when you cursed at her?"

Ricky: "I wanted to tell her that she hurt my feelings, but I didn't. I always think about what I *should* have said after everyone leaves! So if you want to know what I'm thinking right now, wait 'til we're finished with time-out and when we're walking back to class, then I'll tell you."

Ricky was a caring, sensitive, easily frustrated student who had a poor sense of his own identity. Ricky lived with his mother, to whom he felt overly attached and emotionally obligated. Frequently he did not attend school so he could stay home and console his mother as she battled a severe and chronic depression.

When Ricky perceived his mother as being too close, he felt trapped and feared that he would lose his identity. Conversely, when he perceived his mother as being too distant — such as when she talked about suicide — he became anxious because of the implied abandonment. Typically, Ricky reacted to the threat of being too close or too distant by physically or verbally punishing himself. Any anger that he may have felt toward others was turned inward by hitting himself, or making himself physically ill through violent crying.

At school, Ricky's self-destructive manner perpetuated his difficulties. Some staff were demoralized by his pattern of self-destructiveness and would become emotionally rejecting. Ricky used these negative responses to confirm his sense of inadequacy. One problem was that Ricky gravitated to students and staff that replicated his relationship with his mother. In short, he reacted to others in the same way that he reacted to his mother. In time-out, the goal was to help him break the cycle by helping him to slow down his thinking process so he could recognize the feelings that gave rise to his self-destructive behavior.

When I asked Ricky to confront his conflicted feelings, he facetiously told me that he was unsure if he could ever bring a spontaneous manner to sharing his feelings. However, he would try his best, even if the process were somewhat delayed. I would like to think that slowing down the process would gradually help Ricky to achieve greater spontaneity. A school staff that models spontaneous and non-defensive behavior helps to create an atmosphere in which students like Ricky are more likely to talk about their feelings rather than acting out in a destructive manner.

67. STEVE: *California*

Steve had an older brother who had also gone to the school some years earlier. Steve and his brother were both very bright, but his brother was anti-social, stealing cars and committing other felonies. Steve was not anti-social, and his affection for his brother caused him to have some conflicted feelings.

Now, Steve's older brother had gone to jail. I overheard some other students asking Steve about his brother. He answered, "He's in California." Knowing the truth of the matter, I took him aside and asked him about it.

Me: "Steve, why are you telling everyone that your brother is in California?"

Steve: "Well, he *is* in California — 26th and California!" (The Cook County jail is located at 26th Street and California Avenue in Chicago.)

To preserve his brother's privacy, Steve kept a secret which he embedded in a distortion. When we discussed the incident, Steve said he would have felt guilty if he had disclosed to his peers that his brother was in jail. Over time, Steve talked with his social worker about the implications of the conflicted feelings he had about his brother. For example, the image of his brother in jail represented the bad self-image Steve had when he was tempted to break rules at school or at home. Moreover, Steve felt that betraying his brother would undermine his relationship with his mother. Steve's revelations to the social worker helped him to expand his awareness of the meaning of the tale.

68. BRANDON: *Brandon's Choice*

Brandon had been in our school for quite a few years, coming in at elementary school, and going on through junior high school. As bright and insightful as he was, his emotional difficulties continued to get in the way. It was not possible to mainstream him successfully back into the public school system.

Brandon was preparing to go from junior high into high school, but still having significant emotional and behavioral problems. He did not get along well with his teacher at that time. He frequently complained about her, even though she provided a lot of special food rewards, such as candy and pop, for good behavior and good school work.

As Brandon was about to enter high school, we discussed his anger toward his present teacher, and also his new teacher, to whose high school class Brandon was going to be assigned. His new teacher was known for her sweet, supportive manner and for being very easy to get along with — much more so than his present teacher — but she was never known to bring treats into the classroom. I asked Brandon:

Me: "Would you rather have the comfort and support of a friendly teacher when you go into high school, or would you prefer to have tangible, material food rewards like your current teacher provides?"

There was a long pause.

Me: "Brandon, what are your thoughts about that?"

Brandon: "I'm ... *thinking!*"

(Reminiscent of Jack Benny's famous line, when accosted by a robber who gave him the choice, "Your money or your life!")

Brandon was a ward of the state who was removed from his home due to physical abuse and emotional neglect. Once he was removed from his biological parents, he expected others to make up the difference for his difficult past. When others did not meet his demands, he felt angry and rejected. Tangible rewards such as food became his "lifeline" for emotional and physical gratification.

Brandon's present teacher, although gruff, supplied tangible gratification with sweets and treats, which seemed to fill the void he felt inside of himself. On the other hand, the kind and caring high school teacher symbolized the emotional closeness of which he was deprived. But it was difficult for Brandon to commit to it, given his fear of being hurt and rejected. Brandon's hesitation in answering communicated the difficulty he felt in choosing between his hopes and his fears. His "hope" was for someone to support and nurture him — to be the "good parent" he never had. His "fear" was that he would be rejected and hurt by anyone who offered the promise of love, but instead turned out to be the "bad parent" he had.

In this tale, Brandon's indecisiveness was funny on the surface. But rushing someone into a quick answer, without insight, does not promote self-awareness. We find aspects of ourselves scattered in many of the students. Brandon's indecisiveness is more than just the tale of one boy. It has meaning for anyone who has felt rushed into making an important decision that is influenced by underlying factors that are too threatening to acknowledge. In this light, it is important to avoid cornering students into answering questions prematurely. The answer they give is less important than encouraging them to ask questions about themselves, which stimulates introspection.

69. RYAN: *Playground Rules*

Ryan was in time-out for verbally threatening a teacher while on the playground.

Me: "What happened?"

Ryan: "You said it was okay!"

Me: "I said *what* was okay?"

Ryan: "You said it was okay to curse on the playground!"

Me: "When did I say that?"

Ryan: "Once, when I cursed in class you said that type of language was for the playground!"

Ryan, age 8 years old, had particular difficulties with self-control. When he felt stressed or rejected, his tendency was to display intense, angry or aggressive feelings. But behind the façade of hostility, Ryan was a scared little boy who tried to be good enough to deserve his mother's attention and love. Waiting for emotional support that never came, Ryan developed a black-or-white picture of adults — they were either despicable and unworthy of his respect, or charming and admirable. In either case, adults ended up being a caricature of themselves in his eyes. His lack of balance in perceiving adults in a realistic manner provided intense feelings of either adulation or alienation.

Ryan's slippery slope of volatile thoughts led some of his peers to be dismissive of his exaggerated viewpoints, which in turn triggered increased feelings of rejection and stress. Ryan needed someone to blame for his quick temper. Removing his complicity for cursing at the teacher was one way to re-frame his verbal outburst as being "legitimate." On one level, Ryan used a coping strategy such as "blaming" to drive a wedge between himself and adults. He wanted to expose their shortcomings even if the underlying purpose was to avoid acknowledging his own feelings of being "unworthy."

In working with Ryan, I learned that thought-based, rather than feeling-based, questions improved his chances for recovery. For example, by asking Ryan what would happen if it turned out that it was not *my* fault — for giving him 'permission' to curse on the playground — helped him to assess his own thinking process. While some may argue that in time-out students need to explore their feelings first, and reason later, for Ryan, exploring his feelings was possible only after he had been engaged in reasoning about what happened. Having first-hand knowledge of Ryan's thinking process helped me to ask questions that improved his chances for recovery in time-out.

70. EARL: *A Therapeutic Moment*

Earl was a 15-year-old boy who had been at the school for several years after being referred to the school from juvenile court. He was involved in many anti-social activities and had been in time-out many times due to aggressive behavior in class. This tale, however, occurred when he was at home.

Earl lived in a single-parent home with his mother and an aunt. On one occasion, Earl wanted to leave the house late at night, and his mother blocked the door. Later, when his mother got dressed to go out, he blocked her and said she couldn't leave either! He became physically aggressive to keep her from leaving the house. His aunt called the police, and when they arrived, they found Earl sitting on his mother.

Police: "What's going on here?"

Earl: "My mother and I are having a therapeutic moment."

Earl was 15 years old and presented himself with a grandiose sense of importance. He perceived himself as brilliant and special, and felt that he could be understood only by other brilliant and special people. In class and at home, Earl's hostile, verbal and aggressive attacks on others said more about his own need to be defiant than they did about the individuals he attacked. Earl was trying to rigidly organize his own perceived superior status around illusions of being better than others.

Sometimes one's persona can be framed by a single event. In this tale, Earl's actions and comments are an apt metaphor for an individual whose self-importance is so strong that when his personal desires are not gratified, he becomes enraged and feels entitled to lie and act out. His personal motto seemed to be, "Neither my mother nor the police have a right to stop me from doing anything I want to do." For Earl, the feeling of entitlement to special treatment was rooted in part in his belief that his intelligence exempted him from rules which others must follow.

There is a significant distinction between students who resist authority in order to camouflage their own perceived inadequacies, and students like Earl, who overestimate their own importance and view their intelligence as a justification for defying legitimate authority. Students who view themselves in a self-righteous and guiltless manner tend to respond negatively in their counseling sessions. Earl was comfortable with his beliefs about how to get along with others. As a result, he was quick to take exception to suggestions about his behavior. Earl felt that he might lose claim to special privilege if he did not present himself as being beyond criticism. The counseling goal for Earl was to help him recognize that in moving from anti-social to pro-social behavior, he might realistically heighten his sense of personal significance and prestige.

71. MATT: *No Answer*

Matt had been sent to time-out for becoming frustrated, losing his temper, and tearing up some books in the classroom.

Matt: "Why do I do what I do? I know it's wrong, and I don't want to do it, but I do it anyway. There is no answer for that!"

Me: "Could it be that you are trying to let me know how guilty you feel when you act out in class?"

Matt: "I *knew* it! You have an answer for everything! Even questions that have no answer!"

50 thousand questions

Dr. Henry Roth
NAME
Has completed the astounding feat of producing:
50,000 Answers

to

50,000 Questions
that have NO ANSWER!

Phil Ossifer, Ph. D.

December 1, 2008
ON THE DAY OF

Matt was a 16-year-old boy who was insecure about his academic abilities, and ridiculed others that he perceived to be more capable than himself. Matt's mother was physically disabled, and his father left to Matt the task of taking care of her. The pressure of this responsibility left Matt feeling guilty for not doing enough to help her. This dynamic further reinforced his sense of inadequacy. At school, he tried to overcome his fear of being academically inept by demonstrating that others were inept for not knowing the answers to *his* questions. By asking questions no one could answer, he reversed a "one-down" to a "one-up" situation in which he had the advantage.

In this tale, Matt had difficulty exploring his guilty feelings, and he reframed my question as an absurdity. His humor transformed feelings of vulnerability into feelings of power. From his point of view, his comments exposed the foolishness of an authority figure who presumed to ask useful questions that would illuminate his guilty feelings. In this manner, he minimized the power of my questions and my authority. His comments seemed to reassure him that I was a harmless person from whom he had nothing to fear. Now, instead of being threatened by my authority or my questions, he was free to laugh at me.

Before I could figure out how to respond, Matt began telling me he was very sorry. When I asked him to tell me more about those feelings, he said he was sorry he couldn't do more for his mother. But he often found himself slipping off to do personal things rather than helping her. Matt felt burdened by his responsibility to his mother while outwardly presenting the impression of being dutiful. Ultimately, Matt told me that the only perfection he could hope for was finding imperfection in others, and he accomplished that by putting others down.

In looking back on this tale, I realize that Matt was correct: I usually answered questions by asking more "exploratory" questions. On the other hand, such questions allow students to process the disturbing impact of their conflicted feelings in a safer and less anxiety-provoking manner. Questions such as, "Can you tell me more about what happened?" or "Have you had other experiences like this?" offer, as Fritz Redl put it, "emotional first-aid," because they help one feel safer in acknowledging the events that lead to time-out encounters.

72. HAROLD: *Harold's Choice*

Harold was in time-out for punching and damaging a bulletin board. His therapist, teacher and mother had been giving him more choices regarding consequences for his misbehavior; so I followed suit and gave him a choice of consequences for damaging the bulletin board.

Me: "Do you want to lose computer privileges, gym or music privileges?"

Harold: "Let's not take any chances. Take away everything."

In this tale, Harold was feeling powerless to control his anger. By asking me to take away "everything," he tried to write a different ending to a time-out episode in which he felt he was no longer in control of the situation or himself. Harold transformed the feeling of losing control into an exaggerated yet funny comment about the intensity of his anger. Now he could experience, even if just for a moment, the comforting thought that he was "in control" of the situation — even though, in this instance, it meant losing all his privileges.

Harold's admonition to me not to take any chances with his anger mirrors the struggle we all face to overcome our angry thoughts and feelings. For many of us, even thinking about our anger means that we might act out in a destructive way. Then this fear is hidden behind defensive maneuvers such as humor. In Harold's case, he used humor as a defense to reverse his feelings of powerlessness. This allowed him to accomplish some short-term advantages — but at the price of losing all his privileges.

It was important for me to look beyond the immediate implications of Harold's comment and focus instead on how his selection of his particular response in time-out was one way for him to give meaning to an upsetting experience. In this manner, Harold could better understand and appreciate the unique way in which a joking manner can both help and hurt one's self-interests.

73. TERRY: *Unchangeable*

Terry: "I hate the way I have to go to time-out at this dumb school."

Me: "It sounds like you want to change the way we do things here?"

Terry: "Not really. I just don't want the school to change *me!*"

Terry was an insular, guarded 16-year-old, who was conflicted about his sexual identity. His need to keep his emotions from coming out freely was rooted in part in his fear that if he spoke spontaneously he might say something that might give himself away. His struggle to find himself was especially difficult because self-recognition might lead to guilt, shame and embarrassment. In fact, Terry felt obligated to acquiesce to the expectations of his parents and friends and to his own critical standards as well. He had a highly developed sense of humor which was essential to understanding his personal dynamics. With his quick wit he was able to live out his desire to be accepted and appreciated for his cleverness. Moreover, jocularity kept Terry from further retreating into his inwardly confusing world.

In individual therapy, when personal issues were pointed out to Terry, he tended to feel threatened; and then he would act out in a defensive manner. Thus, in his first year at our school, meaningful discussions with his therapist were rare, as Terry kept the door closed to his private world. In his second year, Terry gradually reported to his therapist the funny comments he had made in class or in time-out. This became an important way for him to discuss how it gave meaning to his experiences. In so doing, Terry became more spontaneous about expressing his thoughts and feelings.

In Terry's tale from time-out, his teacher told him that his homework was incorrect. He felt threatened that he was unable to perform the task expected of him, and displaced his anger and disappointment with himself onto his teacher by acting in a verbally inappropriate manner. Actually, this was the same critical manner in which his father related to Terry when he was upset with him. In saying, "I just don't want the school to change me," Terry was expressing his fear of being judged. He transformed this fear into an amusing, but accurate assessment of what he was privately feeling.

At the end of his second year, it was still difficult for Terry to sort out his conflicted thoughts and feelings. However, he was less guarded and more likely to take chances. He often fumbled in his search for a blueprint that would help him to shape his identity. At such times, humor served as the compass he needed to direct him as he gradually constructed a more accepting and positive image of himself.

74. FREIDA: *Something In My Pocket*

Freida was in the hallway talking to me, as a student was being taken to time-out by his teacher. He "shot me the finger" as he passed by.

Freida: "How rude! I would never do something like that!"

Me: "Well, lately you have been doing very well at school. Could it be that there were times in the past when you felt like making that gesture?"

Freida: "Well, yes — I felt like it sometimes — but at least I left my finger in my pocket!"

Freida was a funny and sensitive 16-year-old from a troubled single-parent home with her father after her mother had passed away. Her father had a menacing personality and a history of anti-social behavior. Freida's older sister, Mary, would pick fights with Freida when she refused to take the blame for crimes that Mary had committed. On more than one occasion, Mary beat her up in retaliation for refusing to be her partner in crime.

Freida was regularly rewarded with approval from her family when she followed their anti-social model. When she refused to do their bidding, however, they challenged her loyalty and became angry and threatening. Withdrawing their love and support caused Freida to experience intense anxiety and isolation. It was ironic that Freida's refusal to follow her family's anti-social model subjected her to the kind of treatment that is usually reserved for family members who act out anti-socially. Freida tried to satisfy her unmet need for recognition and acceptance at home by acting out passive-aggressively at school. For example, she perpetrated contemptuous verbal attacks on her teachers, and by doing so, she would divert attention from her own feelings of unworthiness and obtain approval from her peers.

Freida's remark, "I left my finger in my pocket," triggered a discussion with me about how her funny comment provided a snapshot of her behavior at school. We speculated that her comment revealed her self-image as a good, but angry, girl who, when she compared herself to others, never really acted out. Freida related this tale from time-out to her counselor. She told the therapist, "I really want to shoot my finger at my family, because they expect me to break all the rules; but I don't do that because I know it would only make things worse. All I can do is keep my finger in my pocket and save my family and myself from how I really feel. I guess the angry girl I try to avoid being at home, I become at school." By acknowledging and ascribing meaning to her own funny comment, Freida gained the strength to change her perception of herself.

75. MRS. MANNING: *The Phone Call*

While in time-out with a youngster who was being physically violent, throwing punches at me and the other crisis worker, I inadvertently hit the "Redial" button on my cellphone. The last call I had made was to Mrs. Manning, the mother of a student.

Later, I received a call from Mrs. Manning. She recognized my phone number on her Caller ID and wanted to let me know that some student had gotten hold of my phone and was making obscene phone calls. I asked her for the details.

Mrs. Manning: "They were grunting and breathing heavily into the phone, and there was cursing in the background!"

Me: "I'm really sorry, Mrs. Manning, but that was no student grunting and breathing heavily — that was *me!*"

Sometimes I feel that parents like Mrs. Manning have a somewhat distorted view of me since their child may report more of what happens in crisis situations where the possibility for ambiguity and confusion is greater than the possibility for clarity and closure. Moving back and forth between my roles as crisis worker and principal involves changing behavior, language and attitude. However, playing the two different roles provides some unexpected advantages. For one thing, it allows me to excuse myself from making a mistake in one role, by thinking, *Well, I'm really good in the other role.* But whether the parent ultimately idealizes or demonizes the effort is not the criterion that determines success or failure. There cannot be an expectation for each parent to value your work. It is useful to hope for the best, develop realistic expectations, and prepare for anything!

76. CHAD: *A Job to Do*

Chad: "I can't make it in Ms. Smith's class."

Me: "I hear your frustration, but it will take time. You have only been in Ms. Smith's class for three weeks. I can't eliminate your frustration, but I can work with you so the feelings you have do not get in the way of doing your job at school."

Chad: "Well, I'm glad you know how to do your job — but I'm just a student here, I don't have a job!"

Time-out highlights the disconnect between comments that are designed to be positive, and the intensity of the student's conflicted feelings. Chad's chronic anger at the school was rooted in part in having to attend a school where he felt stigmatized by his siblings and his neighborhood peers. From Chad's point of view, the very principal who was supposed to prepare him for a return to public school was now in time-out with him, offering nothing more than positive, but empty, rhetoric.

Chad's declaration that as a student, he did not have a "job" is a useful reminder that even when a therapeutic day school is doing its job, for students like Chad, it is difficult to counteract the compelling stigma of attending a specialized school. If we decide to take the risk of "labeling" students and placing them in a specialized school, we should make sure that the placement is appropriate, and that it is used for developing effective intervention strategies. Anything less cannot do justice to a student like Chad, who struggles on a daily basis to overcome his feelings of stigmatization.

77. PAULA: *Reversal of Fortune*

Paula was a very bright 15-year-old girl who began to show signs of initiating time-outs in order to have one-to-one conversations with me. When this pattern began to emerge, I just waited for the next crisis call on my cell phone — never a long wait — to call in a replacement.

Me: "Paula, I'm going to have to leave now. I'll call Mr. Lincoln to stay with you for the remainder of your time-out."

Paula: "Oh, no! *Not Mr. Lincoln! Anybody but Mr. Lincoln!*

Me: "Why? What's wrong with Mr. Lincoln?

Paula: "Dr. Roth! Have you ever sat with that man? He's *so depressing!"*

I made a point of calling in Mr. Lincoln for future sessions. Paula's time-out episodes diminished significantly after that.

Students may suddenly start to show an increased pattern of behavior problems requiring more frequent time-outs. Once in time-out, though, they may quickly settle down and engage in conversation. If it becomes apparent that they simply enjoy conversing on a one-to-one basis, and find time-out more desirable than doing their schoolwork, other alternatives need to be considered.

Paula, age 11, was ashamed and afraid of her father's volatile temper and his abusiveness toward her mother. At school, Paula was silent about her family problems, but she looked depressed. She found fault with most males, both adults and children. Too often, a student's external complaints are treated at face value, while the underlying issue is unrecognized and untreated. In Paula's case, the problem was acknowledging depression in someone who was unable to face her own desperate circumstances.

Paula's perception of Mr. Lincoln as "so depressing" was a mirror into her own private world of sadness. At times, Paula used her depression to gain a temporary edge on battling the everyday pressures she experienced. For example, she once asked me in time-out, "Don't you think it's kind of cool that everyone is always waiting for me to start crying?" Paula tried to strike terror into the hearts of others so she could avoid striking out in terror toward her father.

Manipulation, like humor, can be used in response to extreme stress. Paula's manipulation was reinforced by all the attention and interest she received, in part from me. It was necessary to be careful to avoid legitimizing Paula's manipulations, which enabled her to evade stressful situations, such as doing her schoolwork. Depression and manipulation feed on each other. In cases such as Paula's, when both are present, both must be acknowledged and treated.

78. CLARK: *Super-Hero*

Clark was a 9-year-old boy who liked to mimic superhero characters from the comic books. Other students often became irritated with these antics. Ultimately, he would become angry, curse uncontrollably, and often end up in time-out. On one occasion, I entered the time-out room to relieve a crisis worker who had been with him for some time.

Clark: "Oh no! Not you again, Dr. Roth! Why don't you just f--- off!"

Me: "I'll be patient with you, Clark, until you are more relaxed and can return to class."

Clark (in a deep growling voice): "Grrrrrrr-eat! while you're being patient with me can I tell you to f--- off one more time?"

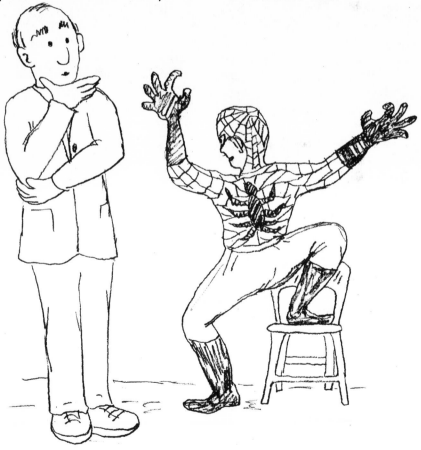

Significant traumatic losses in his early life contributed to the inappropriate manner in which Clark related to others. At age six, he was removed from his home due to chronic maltreatment. In the first grade, Clark demonstrated significant behavioral problems. He was frequently absent from school and spent most of his time at his foster home watching TV cartoons or reading super-hero comic books.

Clark was referred to our school at the age of eight. During his first year at the school, his imitations of cartoon characters lasted for at least ten minutes, several times a day. During these episodes, Clark would pretend to fly, or climb the walls, and sound or act like a fantasy figure. His teacher created a warm and supportive classroom environment, and tried to avoid punitive consequences at these times. She felt that strategies organized solely around consequences were not likely to be maintained or generalized. Instead, she looked for opportunities to understand what triggered his cartoon-like enactments, prior to their occurrences.

Clark was typically vague about identifying a triggering event. His teacher tried to raise questions that could help him find meaning in his enactments. She challenged Clark to think about asking additional questions about his own behavior and how he could answer them. Clark's first impulse was to find almost any excuse for his behavior, such as, "I just felt like it," or, "I don't know." He wanted to dismiss exploratory questions as ridiculous, and became annoyed if they were pursued. In spite of many discussions with him, he had no real understanding of why he acted the way he did. Gradually, Clark was able to acknowledge that perhaps there was some meaning to his need to imitate cartoon characters.

The healing process appeared to begin when Clark recognized that his teacher, and other staff, listened to him more carefully than he listened to himself. It was out of this process that Clark disclosed that ever since he could remember, he believed that no one was really interested in him, and that he preferred his cartoon characters to the real world. He did not see how he could defend himself from uncaring adults without the help of a super-hero who would be there to protect him. Ralph Waldo Emerson said, "We live amid surfaces and the true art of life is to skate well on them." Once Clark was able to see beneath the surfaces, he was better able to skate well on top of them.

STRATEGIES FOR TIME-OUT

STRATEGIES FOR TIME-OUT

Even the most stable person wrestles with inner conflicts. When faced by a student in time-out who has minimal self-control, we can all understand how difficult it is for him to restore his emotional equilibrium. The student's struggle in time-out mirrors the struggle that everyone faces to hold back powerful emotions long enough to be able to say or do the right thing.

Before sending a student to time-out, staff should attempt to reinforce positive behavior. They may utilize a variety of interventions that set students up for staying in the classroom, rather than requiring removal to time-out areas. Such interventions may include humor, encouragement, physical proximity (such as moving closer to the student's desk), and patiently presenting reasonable choices. Nevertheless, under the best of circumstances, problematic behavior can escalate to the point of explosiveness or violence.

The primary indicator for placing a student in time-out is to protect the student from harming himself or others. Secondary indicators for utilizing time-out include preventing significant property damage, and avoiding chaos in the classroom. It is also reasonable to take a student to time-out who requests to be taken, and has over time exhibited an accurate anticipation of an approaching loss of his own control.

The following suggestions attempt to identify specific approaches that can contribute to an accepting atmosphere in time-out. In this type of environment, students are more likely to use humor as a metaphorical expression of their unacknowledged and disturbing feelings.

ANALYZING HUMOR

Use caution in analyzing humor and making categorical judgments. The concealed message in a capricious comment should only be interpreted if it seems indicated. In most cases it is more useful to highlight themes or triggers. By not focusing on the direct meaning of the comment, one reveals an appreciation of the student's need to avoid facing his own disturbing feelings at that moment. A student who is *not* receptive to discussing his facetiousness is, to paraphrase Oliver Wendell Holmes, "Like the pupil of the eye — the more light you pour upon it, the more it will contract."

Respecting the power of comedy to externalize tension and protect students from prematurely experiencing their explosive feelings can prevent further erosion of their shaky self-esteem. Of course, the goal is to have the student face his feelings. But the process of first dealing indirectly with the comment in an empathic manner helps students to feel comforted and understood, and therefore lessens their anxiety during stressful encounters. Unfortunately, it is easy to examine humor in a manner that reflects one's own values or confirms pre-determined thoughts, which may turn out to be inaccurate.

EFFECTIVE INTERPRETATIONS

If the concealed message in a funny comment is interpreted, a student's reaction following the interpretation can validate or invalidate its effectiveness. Generally, reactions to interpretations revolve around the theme of improvement. If the student replies in a positive manner about improving himself (as "Simcha" did at the end of Tale No. 11), it can be viewed as a confirmation of the validity of the interpretation. Conversely, a hostile reply that the interpreter or someone else needs improvement (as "Kramer" did at the end of Tale No. 56), can be viewed as a confirmation that the interpretation is off-target. Even if accurate, the interpretation may have been too threatening at that point in time to be integrated. Thus, an effective interpretation can lead to positive and clever reactions, where the student recognizes the need to fix or improve himself. On the other hand, an ineffective interpretation can lead to negative or sarcastic reactions, where the student attempts to fix or improve the interpreter.

 ## JUDGMENTAL COMMENTS

Avoid direct or implied judgmental comments. In time-out, such comments may be perceived by the student as a retaliatory weapon rather than a helpful suggestion. They undermine chances for de-escalation. Examples of judgmental comments include, "How could you say such a thing?" or, "That wasn't even funny," or, "Don't you realize how inappropriate that was?" On the other hand, non-punitive, non-threatening, non-moralistic language helps to avoid getting drawn into an escalating power struggle. Examples include comments like, "Are there other ways you can express your strong feelings without so much anger?"

What is essential is an adult who can accept a student's need to use provocative wit without becoming threatened into responding in a counterproductive manner. Reasonable flexibility on the part of the staff provides a model for the type of restraint that you hope the student will eventually display in managing his own intense feelings.

 ## EMPATHIC ATMOSPHERE

It is essential to provide an empathic atmosphere in which the student can process his hurt feelings. A student may use hostile sarcasm to blame the teacher for everything that happened, not realizing that he is attacking the teacher for failings of his own. Staff should not view the sarcasm as falsifying reality. Rather, it should be seen as revealing important impressions that powerfully shape behavior. In this type of framework, chances for the student's recovery are enhanced. Empathy and the good will it inspires can be just as important as an accurate understanding of the disturbing events which led to the time-out.

"THE EXCITEMENT OF NOT KNOWING"

When jazz saxophonist Johnny Griffin was asked the meaning of "improvisation," he replied, "The excitement of not knowing!" Similarly, in reacting to a student's playfulness, well-practiced and sterile comments can interfere with what our intuition might otherwise tell us. A spontaneous and genuine approach can resonate more directly with the student, rather than "playing by the book." The point is not just the content of what is said, but the attitude with which the staff person approaches the student's comments.

 THE SILENT STUDENT

The following approaches can be useful in helping students who won't talk in time-out to become more verbal and spontaneous. First, one can ask for suggestions instead of information. For example, rather than asking "What seems to be wrong?" or, "Why aren't you talking?" one might say, "I'm concerned that you are not talking. What would be some helpful ways for us to begin to talk with each other?" In this manner, the staff person is seeking information in a way that makes it easier for the student to feel comfortable about exploring the issues that triggered the time-out. Re-framing the silence in a positive light helps to defuse the resistance.

Second, rather than trying to pressure a student into talking, it helps to acknowledge that he may have important reasons to remain silent. Nonetheless, he can talk about these reasons — and what might happen if he decided to reveal his thoughts. Also, it is important to differentiate what students can talk about from what they cannot. They may not be able to talk about everything, but they may be able to define certain "safety zones" which they can freely discuss. In this way, it is possible to develop a record of discrete verbal interactions that strengthen a student's ability to regroup in time-out.

AVOIDING ANGER

In time-out the crucial balance is between seeing the bigger picture (underlying dynamics) and seeing the details (trigger). While it is impossible to strike a perfect balance, the first step is to avoid letting personal feelings interfere with professional behavior. Working with angry students can give staff practice in controlling their own emotions. Handling those feelings effectively, when the first impulse is to get angry can be a rewarding and invaluable experience.

During time-out, the "strategies" invoked and the questions asked are important; but avoiding an angry, stressed-out appearance is just as important. A calm and relaxed manner seems to move a student to restore his emotional equilibrium almost as much as the words that are said. An angry or harsh manner is like a talking animal — what the animal has to say isn't nearly as important as the fact that it's a talking animal.

A congenial presence shows a student in crisis that you value him as a person and do not see him as yet another burdensome frustration. Unless the student feels valued, he may use sarcasm or bursts of temper to communicate his anger that he is not being valued or respected. The student's underlying critique of the staff person's demeanor — concealed behind a flurry of hostile aggression — can be a useful reminder to smile and be more relaxed. It is easier for students to learn how to handle their own anger if they have a model of an adult who is capable of handling his anger.

 VISUAL VS. VERBAL TECHNIQUES

Some students who frequent time-out may have language problems or a limited vocabulary that hinders their ability to express their thoughts and feelings verbally. Others may feel too threatened or uncomfortable to share their feelings with unfamiliar crisis staff. For students who present these challenges, feelings may be better elicited by asking them to draw a picture. Drawing becomes an important way to communicate emotions and classroom events which were previously too difficult to verbalize, (such as "Ronnie" did in Tale No. 25).

The visual images contained in drawings provide an expressive language for explaining the experience that led to the time-out, reminding the student what happened, and "articulating" his unspoken beliefs and attitudes regarding it. What cannot be talked about may be drawn in a manner consistent with the student's level of comfort. Given this alternative technique, the student may experience a sense of control over his disturbing feelings and his reactions to them.

By wrestling with vivid images, students find a way to give meaning in symbolic form to their unspoken thoughts and feelings. They know that words are not the only window into their inner world. Drawing about experiences that led to time-out can reduce a student's stress and anxiety, depending on the unique characteristics of the situation.

An alternative behavioral explanation for the advantages of drawing is that the drawing may desensitize the student to the negative classroom experience through visual exposure to the disturbing event. In this context, extinction of an inappropriate behavior is more likely to occur when it is visualized.

 CIRCULAR LOGIC

Students in time-out view incidents from their own perspectives, and partial vision yields partial truth. As a result, the overall process in time-out involves making connections between distorted facts, intense emotions and complex triggers. That said, the process is far removed from logical reasoning or thinking. To paraphrase Victor Frankel, the role played by therapeutic staff is more like the role played by an eye doctor than that of a painter: "A painter tries to convey a picture of the world as he sees it; an eye doctor enables us to see the world as it really is." The role of staff at a therapeutic school is to help students by broadening their visual field. In that manner, students become more conscious of misdirected, simplified or distorted comments.

In fulfilling the role of Frankel's "eye doctor," it is important for staff to avoid seeing everything the student says as a distortion, even if it appears that way. Students can fail to recognize missteps that seemed clear to them at the time, but that could only be revealed by asking the right questions. Although the student's logic contains a different standard of proof than the norm, there is a kernel of truth in it that should not be dismissed just because the "facts" are stated in an illogical manner. While it is productive to look out for errors in a student's thinking process, it is more productive to view their errors as incomplete statements awaiting elucidation. Thus, a student's cognitive lapse can be viewed as a kernel of truth that needs to be extracted from the shell of circular logic.

THE BEST FIRST QUESTIONS TO ASK

- What brings you to time-out?
- What do you think is the problem?
- What do you think is wrong?
- How can I best help you?

These open-ended types of questions help to reduce the student's anxiety, and that makes it easier for him to answer the more provocative questions regarding the presenting problem. This is similar to medical doctors beginning a physical exam by asking, "Where does it hurt?" then starting their exam some distance away, gradually approaching the painful area. Answers given by students in a state of anxiety or anger are likely to be more defensive and less likely to be an accurate reflection of what actually happened. When they are more relaxed, their responses are more likely to approximate the actual circumstances of what happened.

QUESTIONS TO ASK ONESELF

In time-out, it is often helpful for staff to use the "STAR strategy" to monitor their own responses, as was attempted with "Abe" (Tale No. 6). After stopping and thinking about what happened, and before responding, it is important to try to assess each situation by asking the following questions:

- What **S**trategy would be most helpful to implement?
- Is one's own **T**one positive or does it reflect frustration or anger?
- Is the **A**lliance with the student strong enough to enable the strategy to work?
- Is the strategy **R**ight for this student under the specific circumstances?

 SENSE OF HUMOR

Use your own sense of humor — it can be a critical tool in the face of a student's resistance and anger. A humorous comment can defuse an emotionally intense encounter. It can convey an understanding of the student's need to have a mature role model who can be relaxed and spontaneous in the midst of a crisis.

Students respond better to staff who can deal with physical or verbal aggression without becoming threatened or pushed into a rigid or stereotypical posture. Students in crisis need someone who is not silly, nor whose rigidity cuts them off from appreciating the value of wordplay. Silliness can be misinterpreted as patronizing or mocking; and rigidity can be misinterpreted as "just another uptight adult" who is only interested in maintaining his authority.

On the other hand, someone who uses levity appropriately conveys the message that the crisis can be successfully navigated. Humor serves as a legitimate benchmark for healthy behavior by fostering a supportive and relaxed atmosphere.

Above all, *don't lose your sense of humor!*

Henry J. Roth, Ph. D., has been the Executive Director of the Sonia Shankman Orthogenic School at the University of Chicago since 2005. Before that, he was the Principal of the Jewish Children's Bureau Therapeutic Day School since moving to Chicago, Illinois, in 1989. He was Principal of the Duke University Child Psychiatry Day School, from 1977-1989, and a Clinical Associate Professor with the Duke University Department of Psychiatry.

Henry has been an Adjunct Faculty member in the Department of Special Education at Northeastern Illinois University and the National-Louis University in Chicago. He has published more than sixty articles in the area of working with child and adolescent students with emotional and behavioral problems, as well as a textbook that focuses on Orthodox religious students with special needs, *Climbing Jacob's Ladder: Teaching and Counseling Orthodox Students*. His wife, Lorraine, also painted the illustrations for that book.

Henry was born in Chicago and resides with Lorraine in the Chicago area. They have three children and two grandchildren.

Also by Henry J. Roth, Ph. D...

Climbing Jacob's Ladder: Teaching and Counseling Orthodox Students

Written with the compassion and sensitivity of a talented therapist, teacher and administrator, Dr. Henry Roth has integrated key principals of psychology, education and religion in a clear, well organized manner. The religious narratives provide an excellent example of the importance of the interplay between religion and psychology — a main thesis of this wonderful book. The book is also enhanced by the warmth and peacefulness of paintings by the author's wife, Dr. Lorraine Roth. *Climbing Jacob's Ladder* is a comprehensive, insightful and most practical book which will enhance the work not only of those working with orthodox students but also anyone working in a mainstream school setting.

> —Neil J. Fialkow, M. D.
> Child and Adolescent Psychiatrist and Consultant to the Jewish Child & Family Services of Chicago.

===

Dr. Roth's book fills a need in literature for educating orthodox students with emotional problems complicated by religious obligations. The book is clearly written and well-organized, with many real case examples and useful snapshots of children. Dr. Roth also sprinkles his text with many compelling religious examples that beautifully illustrate his message.

> —Janet W. Lerner, Ph. D.
> Author and Professor Emeritus of Special Education, Northeastern Illinois University, Chicago.

===

Dr. Roth's book is a treasure trove of approaches and techniques for complex issues: the overlap of religion, ethics, behavioral and emotional issues, family systems, training of teachers and clinicians, and the paradoxes of supervision and administration. Freud said that teaching and therapy were "impossible professions." This book shows that it is not only possible, but can be done skillfully, humanely and with excellent results.

> —Fred W. Steffen, L. C. S. W.
> Associate Executive Director
> Jewish Child & Family Services of Chicago

==

Some youngsters who feel that they cannot hold their own in the school environment may take out their anger by rebelling against their parents and the religion that put them there. Dr. Roth has made a thorough study of the problems that are encountered in therapeutic day schools. *Climbing Jacob's Ladder* is essential reading for all educators, and is equally important for parents.

> —Rabbi Abraham J. Twerski, M. D.
> Hasidic Rabbi, Psychiatrist, Author, Founder and
> Medical Director of Gateway Rehabilitation Center in
> Pennsylvania.

==

Dr. Roth has written this analysis with a clear sense of devotion, dedication and love for his students and a wonderful sense of humor that makes this book both readable and enjoyable. I commend this book most highly and encourage every educator and parent who wishes to be sensitive to the needs of our children to read this book and learn its lessons.

> —Rabbi Harvey A. Well, Ph. D., Superintendent
> Associated Talmud Torahs of Chicago